ORDINARY GUY, EXTRAORDINARY GOD

GARY F FENLON

Penwick
PRESS

Ordinary Guy - Extraordinary God

By Gary Francis Fenlon

© Copyright 2020 Gary F. Fenlon
Published by Penwick Press

Connect with the author on facebook at: Gary F. Fenlon.

ISBN:978-0-9994311-3-9

Cover design by sarahfenlonfalk.com and cheriefox.com

Interior design by sarahfenlonfalk.com

❀ Created with Vellum

In memory of Alma Fenlon and Mildred Aldrich,
my mother and my mother-in-law respectively,
both of whom greatly impacted my life
through the example of their prayer-lives
and their faithfulness to our God.

FOREWORD

Dear Reader,

Grace and peace to you, from God our Father, the Lord Jesus Christ, and the Holy Spirit who lives inside each believer.

The purpose of this book is twofold. First and foremost, I hope to give glory to our awesome Heavenly Father who never ceases to amaze me! It's amazing to think that the God who created the heavens and the earth desires to have a close relationship with you and I.

Secondly, I want to encourage the average, everyday believer that God can and will use you to accomplish His purposes if you will only make yourself available to Him. Trust God, remain open and enjoy the journey of life. I will ask you questions at the end of each chapter to initiate personal reflection and perhaps even prayer. I hope you find them helpful.

Proverbs 3:5-6: Trust in the Lord with all your heart and lean

not on your own understanding; in all your ways submit to
Him and He will make your paths straight.

I'm writing this book because God told me to. So what you
are reading is God's idea not mine. It was about 2 a.m. one
morning when all of a sudden I was wide awake. God spoke
to me and told me that I would write this book, and then
proceeded to give me the title. At first I kind of laughed, I
have never written much of anything, and especially not a
book. That being said I want to be obedient so you have in
your hands what God told me to write.

This book is about having a relationship with your Heavenly Father through faith and trust in Jesus Christ. It is not a
book about religion. Nor is it a book about theology,
although I will mention some biblical principles as we go
along. Rather, it is an account of the ways that God the
Father, God the Son and God the Holy Spirit became real in
my life and the multitude of ways He has shown Himself to
me and still shows Himself to me in my daily life. I hope you
will be encouraged and inspired to seek Him and find Him
in your own life.

Blessings, Gary F. Fenlon

Luke 1:37 - With God nothing is impossible!

Psalm 31:24 - Be strong and take heart
all you who hope in the Lord.

ACKNOWLEDGMENTS

A special thanks to my beautiful wife, Susan, who always encourages me to try (almost) anything I may never have tried before, like writing a book.

To my children Sarah, Joshua, Jacob and Rebekah, who have probably taught me more than I ever taught them.

A special thanks to our oldest daughter Sarah who helped me whip this book into shape and has helped me publish. She is an example of bravery and boldness. She has fought cancer three times courageously and without being fearful (great concern of course, but not fear.) Joshua 1:9 says: "Be strong and courageous. Do not be afraid, do not be discouraged for the Lord your God will be with you wherever you go."

Sarah has published the account of this journey in Finding Myself ... Facing Cancer as well as five other books now. She took the time to share her knowledge and experience of writing and publishing with me. Thank you, Sarah.

LIFE ON THE FARM

As always, the question is: where to begin? So, I guess I will begin at the very beginning. I was born on September 17, 1951 in Cheboygan, Michigan to Chester and Alma Fenlon. I was the last of their five children. I have two older brothers and two older sisters. I grew up in the country on a small farm near a little place called Alverno. I had a wonderful childhood. Many of these great memories I share with my grandchildren.

One of my grandchildren's favorite memories (the boys anyway) is "the one about the cow pies". If you have not grown up on or around a farm and are wondering what in the world cow pies might be, let me explain. A cow pie is a pile of cow droppings, essentially. But usually after the cow has done its duty and the dung has sat for a while it develops a crust on it, creating the look of a baked pie. Hence the name, cow pie. Now, I'm not really sure if that's where the term came from, but that's the term and the rationale we used to describe it on our farm.

. . .

Alright, so you may be thinking, "What in the world? I picked up this book with a great cover and a great title and this guy is talking about cow dung?"

I know, I know. Stick with me. It really does have a point and as one of my earliest memories is more than just a funny story. I'll continue:

As the story goes (this is all true by the way), it was a beautiful Sunday afternoon and my cousin and I had just returned to my home from church. He lived next door and we were both dressed in our Sunday best, this included a white shirt with a small bowtie and dress slacks. The adults were visiting inside the house and my cousin and I, both about eight to ten years old, were outside goofing around. We decided to go through the gate that kept our cattle inside the pasture, which was near our barn. As we proceeded through the gate we, of course, came across cow pies in our path. As we encountered said cow pies we found some small sticks nearby with which to stab into the cow pies. The problem that arose there was that once breaking through the crust of the cow pie you have a stinky, sticky substance on the end of your stick that you have to flick to get off. (Do you see where this might be going?) When you flick your stick that substance is bound to fly! Then if it is pointed at another person and if it makes contact with that person's white shirt, you really have a problem. Then to compound the problem that person may do the same thing and before you know it, you have what's called a good, old fashioned cow pie fight on your hands! The end result is getting that stinky smelly substance all over your Sunday clothes, in your hair, and etc. Of course, what I described is what actually took place. One thing led to another and before you know it we were covered with cow dung.

If you've gone that far, it won't be long until reality sets in. We knew we were in big trouble! Fortunately, one of my older brothers came outside to find us and of course quickly recognized the trouble we were in. So, he had a bright idea. He would go into the house, open the bathroom window and help us get inside to wash our clothes off one at a time. As you may have guessed, it didn't work out as well as we had hoped and my mom (and others) found out quite quickly what had happened. I think the smell gave it away! To be honest, I don't remember the punishment, but I do remember, it never happened again, at least not in our Sunday best!

I like to tell my grandchildren about riding the pigs too. One particular time I can remember was when I was only about ten years old. The pigs outweighed me ten to one, if not more. We would challenge one another to see who could stay on the pig the longest. It was quite a trick to get on the pig's back and grab an ear and its tail and then hold on for dear life. The ride would usually only last about three to five seconds. Not too bad for a ten-year-old! By the way, this was NOT done with your Sunday clothes on since the pig pen was not the cleanest place to try to ride the pig and inevitably end up in the mud (or worse)!

What do these accounts have to do with our everyday lives?

Even though they may be humorous stories of young kids making poor choices, don't we as adults do the same? Don't we make poor choices and end up figuratively getting our characters soiled by our actions? So, there is a correlation between the two.

Not every remembrance from that time of my life has to do with getting dirty or of the animals themselves. Some of my fondest memories of growing up on the farm came after a long day of work. We had to haul hay from the fields to be stored in our barn. Our barn was on top of a hill overlooking a valley with a creek that emptied into a nearby river. On warm summer days I would sit on the hay once it had been stacked in the barn. I could feel the breeze blow between the cracks of the wood that sided the barn. I remember the sweet smell of the hay and as I looked out a small window that oversaw the valley below, even as a boy, I would wonder about God and life in general. It was here that I would daydream about what I might do with my life, about girls, and of course I would dream about fast cars that I hoped to own one day.

As I grew up here on the farm, known as Fenlon Hill, my summers were mostly carefree. After doing my chores around the farm, an average day would consist of fishing at the local dam, playing softball, riding bikes and picking up bottles and cans so we could turn them in for the deposit and get penny candy. (Yes, you could get candy for a penny back then.) Summer was just about enjoying life as a boy with my friends.

. . .

Life was so simple back then. I went to school in a one-room schoolhouse. "Benton Number Three" I think they called it. It is no longer there, but it was located across from the St. Francis Catholic Church in Alverno. I don't remember a lot about the one-room school other than I had fun with my classmates playing tag and various other youthful games. Yes, life was so simple and enjoyable what now seems a lifetime ago.

How has the way you grew up formed what you believe about God?

ASKING QUESTIONS

I think It was around the age of twelve or thirteen that I became an altar boy and served our priest at St. Francis Church in Alverno. I think my family hoped that one day I too would become a priest. Maybe every good Catholic family back then expected one of their boys to become a priest. I don't know for sure, but I was the last boy standing in the Fenlon family because my older brothers had already married or were intending to get married.

It was during those times serving as an altar boy, attending Catholic catechism classes, and entering Catholic High school, that I really began questioning my faith. I guess I just supposed all teenagers at about that point in life felt the same way and would ask themselves certain questions like: *Is there really a God? If so, what does He want from me? What is life really all about? What am I supposed to do with my life? How can I please God if He truly exists? What happens after I die?*

· · ·

And there were things that happened during this time that caused me to become quite disillusioned with my spiritual life, such as it was. I saw many people who were supposed to be "good Catholics" not living as good people. Even the priests I encountered seemed to fall short of what I thought God must want from His followers. I remember when I was a freshman in high school, one priest invited a group of guys over to his rectory apartment. We were told to make ourselves at home, feel free to have a beer and look through his collection of Playboy magazines. I was appalled at his invitation. To me, this man represented God and if that were the case, how in the world could he be offering beer and pornography to young men?

I saw this hypocrisy in other priests who swore, smoked cigarettes and drank too much. It really turned me off of religion, specifically my religion. I also noticed some of the people that I knew in our small church living in a way that, to me, would not be pleasing to God. To be fair, the same hypocrisy may have been going on in other religions, however I was not involved in other religions at the time so I did not see it. And even in the midst of the hypocrisy there were people living good, godly lives, though the opposite seemed to skew my opinion of the church and of God.

One day after catechism classes I was sitting on the steps of the church waiting for my ride. In that solitary moment I sincerely cried out to God. I said, "God, if you are real, please reveal yourself to me. Otherwise, I'm going to live life my own way." I didn't like what I saw in people and what I was really saying was, "God, I do not want religion, I want a relationship. If you are truly the Living God, I want to know You."

I cannot say there was anything earth shaking that happened at that moment, but somehow, as I looked back a couple of years later, I realized that was a defining moment in my life and it would change my life forever. But before that, for the next couple of years at least, I kind of forgot about that conversation with God on the steps of the church. I was living life like most of my friends. We were all doing what felt good to us like drinking a bit, even though I really didn't care for that. We were chasing girls and driving my dad's car too fast, those were the things I was more interested in at that time. And God took a backseat.

Have you prayed and asked God to reveal Himself to you?

THE DREAM GIRL

Remember I said I was chasing girls and driving fast? Well, my world soon started to change. It happened during my senior year of high school. At that time I attended Cheboygan Catholic High School. (Class of 1969!) My class did spend time during the school day at the public high school taking classes that the Catholic school could not offer. Every day for half a day I would be at the Cheboygan Public High School. One day as I was walking down the hall at the public school I saw a beautiful girl walking in the opposite direction. I was immediately drawn to her. She smiled politely at me as she passed me in the hallway. In that instant God spoke to me and said, "That girl is going to be your wife!"

Now, to this day I cannot explain that. I cannot tell you what God's voice sounded like or how I knew it was Him. All I know is that, in that moment, I knew God was speaking to me. Remember I was not really following God or living life

His way. I was still questioning if in fact there even was a Living God! So, when I heard His voice and it was telling me I was going to marry a beautiful girl I had never met I thought, *I must be going crazy!* I mean, I didn't even know this girl's name! It didn't take me long to find out her name was Susan.

As it turned out I had a couple of classes with her so that was very convenient for me. I got to flirt with her almost every day even if it was only for an hour or so. I also learned that she was quite popular and was dating a guy from the basketball team. That was a problem for me. You see, I was an imposing 5'5" specimen of a young man, weighing in at about 108 pounds my Senior year of high school. While the guy Susan was dating was a 6 foot, blonde haired, blue eyed, 200-pound type. Susan was 5'7" so my thinking was, *why would she give me the time of day, let alone be interested in me in a romantic way?* I began to think that what I had heard in my head (or heart) that day must've been my imagination, not God's voice. After all, I decided, it would take a miracle for this girl to even consider dating a guy like me, not to mention marrying me!

I enjoyed any time I was able to spend in her presence but didn't imagine I had a chance. Then a few months later I heard that she had broken up with the basketball player. Somehow, I got up the courage (after calling and hanging up the phone before it rang about twenty times) to ask her if she would be willing to go to my prom with me, which was coming up in a month or so. She said she would think about it and get back to me. Right. I figured I already knew what the answer was going to be. To my great surprise, she said yes! Then to stun me even more she suggested we go out on a date before the prom to get to know each other better. Wow!

For our first date we went to the movies and I was incredibly nervous, mostly because I was so insecure due to my stature and because she was so gorgeous. At some point on that date she proceeded to tell me that she was still in love with this basketball player. At first this news really bummed me out, but as I would later realize, it turned out to be a blessing in disguise. (I know now God really was at work even though I had no idea at the time). Once she told me that she was in love with another guy, I really relaxed. I remember thinking, "Well good. Now I can just be myself because I've got nothing to lose here." The funny thing is, it turned out that once I relaxed, she very much liked the real me!

Our next date was my Senior Prom. And we had even more dates after that! I remember our first kiss was at my graduation ceremony. I still cannot believe I got up enough nerve to ask for a kiss that day! I thought to myself that so many others were getting kisses from family, friends, as well as girl/boyfriends, that I should take a chance and ask Susan for a graduation kiss. I wouldn't get up that much nerve again for some time. It was about six months before we would have our next kiss.

. . .

I consider getting together with Susan one of the first great miracles in my life! What has God done for you that you have never realized (until now) is a great miracle in your life?

4

MEETING GOD

As we continued dating, I also began attending Susan's youth group meetings at her Lutheran church shortly after my graduation. At first the meetings were just fun and games, social events, but soon they turned into Bible studies.

As we got into Bible study I learned that the God who created the heavens and the earth, wanted to have a personal relationship with someone like me. All I had to do was to seek Him.

It was shortly after the Bible studies began, at seventeen years of age, that I asked Jesus to be the Lord of my life. I can't say I necessarily felt any different in that there was not a lot of emotion or tears, however I knew I was different. I just cannot explain how I knew it. I became what the Bible calls "born again". In John 3:3 Jesus said, "You must be born again to see the kingdom of God."

. . .

This was truly another defining moment in my life. I remember realizing that I was not the same person that I had been the day before. My attitude about myself, about others and about life in general was different in a good way.

Even though I didn't know much of the Bible at that time I later found out that what happened to me is written in 2 Corinthians 5:17: "If anyone is in Christ, they are a new creation, the old (nature) has gone and the new (nature) has come". That was exactly what I had experienced even though I had no idea why. I was amazed that many of the things I had wanted to do the day before I asked Jesus into my life, I no longer wanted to do. I now saw people, especially girls, in a different way. I knew that I needed to treat people in a different and better way. The desire to party was gone and I suddenly realized I had a really bad potty mouth. I knew that needed to change as well.

I could sense a deep hunger for God's word and for the things of God within me. It was then that I remembered what I had told God on the steps of the Catholic Church, "If you are real, I want to know You!"

Suddenly, through the pages of the Reach Out Bible I was given, I started to find God in a real way. I could not put the Bible down. I now found a reason and a purpose to live life each day. I wanted to please my God who loved me enough to send His only Son to die for me. John 3:16 "For God so loved the world (each one of us) that He gave His only begotten Son, that whosoever believes in Him should not perish, but have everlasting life." I knew that scripture was for me as well as for all of mankind. I read through that Reach Out New Testament Bible probably about ten times in the next six months. God's word came alive to me. I learned that God wanted to lead me and guide my life. He loved me enough to send His Holy Spirit to teach me and lead me into all truth. I was in utter amazement at how I started to see my purpose in life was to have a loving relationship with my Creator and loving relationships with other people. Jesus said in Matthew 22:37-39: "Love the Lord your God with all your heart, with all your soul, and with all your mind. This is the first and greatest commandment and the second is like it: Love your neighbor as yourself." As my relationship with God grew so did my relationship with Susan.

Have you met God in a real way in your life?

THE NEXT STEP

As I graduated from high school, the Vietnam War was raging and young men either went to college or faced the possibility of being drafted into the military, unless they joined up first. I had the opportunity to join the Michigan Army National Guard, which had a detachment right in our town of Cheboygan. So, in January of 1970 I left for basic training in Fort Leonardwood, Missouri. It was known as "Fort Lost in the Woods" and rightfully so because it was out in the middle of nowhere! This was a scary time for me. I had never been away from home before and now, on this trip, I was all alone. In fact, this was the first time I had ever flown in an airplane. I remember going through O'Hare airport in Chicago and feeling amazed at how large it was, even back then.

For me this was a time of growing in many ways. I grew spiritually, which may seem odd since I was surrounded by very little having to do with God. I grew physically, which I really needed to do. (Remember I was 5' 5", 108 pounds as I graduated high school.) I also grew in self-confidence, which I also really needed.

After 122 days of boot camp, I had grown 2 inches and put on 20 pounds of pure muscle. I had left home a few months before as a boy and would return a man. Because I was alone and scared I had really cried out to God to help me during this time of training.

Actually, most of the training was pretty easy for me. I could run like the wind, and the classroom work wasn't that hard. The only place I struggled was on the rifle range. As I prepared for the finals for the rifle range, I remember one of my sergeants telling me that even though I had easily passed every other test, I had to pass this one or I would have to start over. I knew I was struggling with accuracy with the rifle and felt shaky. I remember shooting at the first 10 or 12 targets and missing every one of them. I quickly prayed and asked Jesus to help me, nothing special, just a quick cry for help. After that prayer I was able to calm down and I think I only missed another 6 or so shots out of around 140. It *had to be* God because I passed with flying colors.

This event at the rifle range helped me grow in my faith as well as in my self-confidence. I realized I could do almost anything that the military asked of me. Because of my increased confidence and skill I decided to remain in the military and stayed in the Michigan Army National Guard until 1977, reaching the rank of Sergeant E-5. Even though I enjoyed the military for the most part, as our young family grew I felt the National Guard was taking too much time away from them, so I made the decision to end my military career at that point.

When was there a time in your life when you felt all alone? In what ways could you feel God's presence and provision?

COMING HOME

While I was away in basic training I realized just how much I was in love with Susan. Other than God, she was all I thought about day and night. I could not wait to return home and see her again. Even though she wrote me letters everyday I was gone I still missed her terribly. It was my hope and prayer that *she* missed *me* as much as I had missed her. I remember getting off that jet and seeing her for the first time in months. It was like what a piece of heaven must be like. She was so beautiful. I realized that I/we all take so much in life for granted. Life can be short and we need to embrace, enjoy and make the most of every minute of everyday. Being apart from my family and especially from Susan made me realize all of that. I also knew I did not want to spend anymore time apart from Susan.

She did miss me and while I was gone she realized she was in love with me too! I was thrilled. Life was great. I must have asked Susan to marry me one hundred times over the next few months. She finally said yes!

I had returned home at the end of May 1970 and we were

married on February 20, 1971. God is so good! What He had
said to me about two years earlier had come to pass. In my
mind, the fact that this woman would marry me was truly a
miracle that God had done in my life. However, it was not
without its challenges. Remember, I was raised Catholic and
Susan was Lutheran. In those days the two did not mix very
well regarding how each religion, as well as how our families, viewed each other. Also, the priest I had served as an
altar boy under when I was growing up at St. Francis
Catholic Church envisioned me becoming a priest, so it did
not sit well with him either. I spoke with him about having
him take part in our wedding ceremony, which Susan and I
had decided would be held at the Lutheran Church. That
talk did not end well. He told me that he could not do that,
and I would go to hell if I changed religions. I left that
meeting very unhappy with our conversation and
wondering why he had been so harsh. Why was all of this
an issue? Was it such a problem for a Catholic to marry a
Lutheran? Did we not serve the same God?

It was at that time I had made a choice to become
Lutheran because it was at the Lutheran church that I had
experienced a real relationship with the Living God. It was a
difficult decision but I truly felt that was how God was
leading me. Even though I'm sure at the time my family was
not happy with my decision, I had to do what I felt God was
leading me to do.

A most pivotal moment in our wedding planning and
discussions happened just shortly before our wedding. My
grandmother, Lillian, was the matriarch of my family.
And in the midst of all this religious and relational
discord, she went and bought a new dress for our
wedding. It was her way of giving her approval, and the
implication was that the rest of my family should get on

board as well. Unfortunately, about a week before our wedding day she passed away. So most of the family who traveled to Cheboygan for her funeral chose not to travel again only a week later for our wedding. The weather was horrible with an ice storm covering all of northern Michigan that weekend, which also prevented our extended family from coming. The weather was so bad that I had to dig myself out of my brother's driveway that morning.

While we were preparing for the ceremony I was extremely nervous. Susan would later tell me that she was so nervous that her face broke out in hives. She was dressing at the church and I was supposed to go to her house to get dressed. When I got to Susan's house just a short while before the wedding, I arrived to find her father wasn't even dressed yet! He was leisurely sitting at the kitchen table drinking his morning coffee and having his morning cigarette. It made me even more nervous! I urged him to come and get ready and together we fumbled with cummerbunds and ties. There wasn't much to be said as Susan's father wasn't much of a "talker" but together we figured out our outfits and were headed to the church.

We decided upon a traditional Lutheran marriage ceremony. Susan's pastor, Pastor Mantei, conducted the ceremony and we followed his lead in all things. We were so young when we got married (I was nineteen and Susan had just turned eighteen a couple months before) that we didn't include many personal touches, we went along with the program.

There was so much going through my heart and mind the weeks leading up to the wedding and even that morning that I wasn't able to fully reflect on the fact that here I was, living the fulfillment of the words God had spoken to me in that high school hallway, that I would marry this girl. But here I was, marrying that girl! God is faithful!

In the days and weeks that followed our wedding I remember wondering what some of my family thought about me changing religions and so boldly declaring it through our choice of wedding ceremony. I was now much more outspoken about my faith than I ever was as a Catholic. I had come to realize that this life with God was not about what religion I was, but about building a relationship with God. After a few years I think my family realized that I was not just "religious" but that I was sincere in my beliefs and consistent in living my life the best I could for the God I had grown to know and love.

Together Susan and I grew spiritually as our faith in our Lord and Savior went deeper and deeper. God started to use us in the lives of others. He began to do things in our life together that we could have never dreamed.

Are you struggling in a relationship? Trust God to bring peace and provision in the situation.

7

GOD IS GOOD

S oon after we were married, Susan and I went from being members of the youth group at the Lutheran Church to being leaders of it. We had some really blessed times with our Lord and with the members of that group. Years later, as we reflected upon that nucleus of teenagers, we realized that to this day, most of that group are still committed Christians. That is also a miracle in the day in which we live. God is good!

One of the really cool times with the youth group came as we were meeting at our home, a small house trailer on an acre lot near Alverno. We probably had a group of about 12-13 teenagers there, and as we sat on the floor (because there was not enough seating for everyone) in the living room of our house trailer, I remember asking everyone to bow their heads and be silent for just a few minutes. I wanted us to just listen to the Holy Spirit for a bit and see what He would say to us as we gathered there. The next thing I knew an hour had passed. Somehow we had all been so caught up in the Spirit that time almost literally stood still for this group. What seemed like maybe five minutes of silence was actually an hour! Everyone was in amazement how time had gone by so quickly and no one had even moved, stretched, coughed, etc. God somehow touched each person there that day to let them know just how much they were loved by Him.

This reminds of a story I heard once. It goes something like this:

There was a group of young Christians who were wondering why it seems like so many Christians today do not stay committed to following Jesus. Many seem to grow weary of fighting the good fight and fall away. One of them had heard of a man who had committed his life to Christ as a young man and was living a life committed to Christ even in his old age.

This young Christian found out where the old man lived and decided to go and visit him and ask him why he thinks people today fall away from their faith. Soon the young man came upon the old man sitting on his porch in a rocking chair with his dog lying next to him. The young man asked the old man a question: "Sir can I speak with you for a bit?"

"Sure!" the old man replied.

"Well, sir, I have heard that you have been a committed Christian your whole life," the young man said. "Sir, I was wondering if you might have some insight as to why so many today fall away from their faith when you have not?"

"Well," the old man replied, "let me answer your question by telling you a story: One day I was sitting here on my porch with my old hunting dog lying beside me, when suddenly this big white rabbit ran across my yard. Up jumped my dog and off he went chasing that rabbit and barking up a storm. The next thing you know several other dogs, upon hearing my dog, joined in the chase. What a sight it was, a pack of loudly barking dogs running across the fields over the creek and through the brush chasing the big white rabbit. However, after a while one by one the dogs grew tired and frustrated and dropped out of the chase. Finally, there was just one dog left, my old hunting dog. Therein lies the answer to your question young man."

The young man thought for a couple of minutes and then said, "Sir, I'm sorry but I don't see what some dogs chasing a rabbit has to do with people falling away from their faith?"

The old man answered, "Young man, the problem is, you are asking the wrong question. The real question is why did the other dogs give up the chase but my dog did not? The answer to that question is: my dog is the only dog to have *seen* the rabbit."

You see those teens in that youth group had had a real encounter with Jesus and they have never given up chasing after Jesus since. They were not running on someone else's faith or someone else's experience. They were chasing after Jesus because they had, in a sense, "seen" Jesus themselves. Whenever anyone has a genuine encounter with Jesus, then nothing will stop them from following Him for the rest of their lives.

Have you had a genuine encounter with Jesus?

COOL STUFF

While Susan and I were involved with the church youth group another unique opportunity arose. We knew several people who were in on the ground floor of starting a Christian Coffee House in Cheboygan. This was an idea we also had thought and prayed about for some time. We were asked to be a part of it and we jumped at the chance. It was named the Lighthouse Coffee House. There was an old vacant church building on the corner of Division and Dresser streets owned by Citizens National Bank. The bank allowed us to use the facility free of charge. It was located across the street from what we now call "the old Junior High School". We had a staff of about eight to ten Christians, men and women from various churches in Cheboygan. It was a blast! We held Bible studies there, offered a library of books and Christian music and had a foosball table. It was sometimes just a place for kids to come and hang out after school. We even offered live music concerts by Christian individuals or bands most weekends for the community to enjoy.

. . .

I remember when one of the top Christian bands in the US was on tour and they came and played a show at our little coffee house on a Saturday night! The group, Servant, was from out west somewhere but made their way to tiny Cheboygan, Michigan to play for our youth! God is so good! They were awesome. Apparently, they were supposed to do a gig in nearby Traverse City, Michigan but something had happened and that concert fell through. Someone had given them our name as a possible place to play. Wow! I still to this day cannot believe that they played in little Cheboygan at the Lighthouse Coffee House.

Another really cool thing that God did for the Lighthouse Coffee House was during a staff meeting. One of our staff members got a phone call. The call was to inform him that his brother-in-law, who was not a Christian, had suffered a heart attack and was being rushed to the hospital by ambulance. The staff member asked us to pray and hurried off to go to the hospital. We all gathered together and asked God to intervene on this man's behalf. A couple hours later the staff member notified us that his brother-in-law had been *released from the hospital* and the doctors couldn't find anything wrong with him. Praise God! Our staff worker said his brother-in-law hadn't wanted to leave the hospital because he *knew* he had a heart attack and couldn't understand why they were saying there was nothing wrong with him. God is so good!

Being a part of the Christian coffeehouse was enlightening in many ways. Unfortunately, as we learn and grow we can be exposed to the negative side of things as well. Some of these experiences at the Lighthouse opened my eyes to things that greatly concerned me, things that were not so pleasant. Some of the kids that frequented the coffeehouse came from homes that were significantly unstable. One of those kids in particular that comes to my mind as I write this is a young boy, who was probably around the age of 11 or 12. He had stayed at the coffeehouses until closing one night. It was about 1 a.m. and I offered to drive him home.

As I drove near his house, he said, "Keep on going."

I asked him why. He replied, "Well the outside light is not on so that means my mom is still entertaining someone and I cannot come home until the light goes on."

Wow. I may have been a bit naive but I was stunned by what that boy told me. The older I get the more I recognize how the lack of stability in the home is on my mind. I believe this is one of the reasons we have some of the problems we are facing in our country today. Kids are not allowed or able to be kids, and too many of our young people are parenting their parents.

Of course the answer to that problem (as well as to all of life's problems) is, simply put, Jesus. To have healthy relationships and families we need to have God in the middle. In His word He teaches parents how to parent and families how to love and respect one another, to be responsible for themselves and each other. As I always say: there are two ways to live life, our way or God's way, and our way just doesn't work.

Has God recently opened your eyes to concerns you had not been aware of? Pray about them now.

STARTING OUR FAMILY

One of the greatest moments in our lives was on November 7, 1973. This was the day that our first-born, Sarah Julianne, came into this world. It was amazing, but it was not easy! The delivery was not as quick as we would have liked. Susan was in labor for a couple of days, but the wait was worth it. In the midst of our joy, a challenge arose. Sarah was born with a birth defect: meningocele spina bifida. This is when a baby's spinal cord doesn't develop as it should leaving the neural tube open at some point along the spine. Sarah's was on her lower back. Because of this, we could not even bring her home and had to drive four and a half hours to Ann Arbor, Michigan for an operation at Motts Children's Hospital.

We had been married for a short year and a half at this time. As a young, fairly-newly-wed couple this was a great challenge in our lives and to our faith. We were being asked to trust God with an outcome that we dearly hoped for for our beloved firstborn child. I don't remember much about Sarah's time in the hospital or what we were doing as we waited. That time is somewhat fuzzy, those two weeks kind of a blur, but in the end the surgery was successful! Praise God! It felt so good when Sarah was finally able to come home.

Living as a family of three, it didn't take us long to realize we wanted to expand our family. Because of the birth defect Sarah had been born with and my brother's daughter being born with spina bifida as well, the doctors told us another biological child would be a high risk. So, in 1974 we decided to check into adoption. Actually, adoption was something Susan and I had discussed many times before we had any children. Adoption was something we felt God had put on our hearts years before. In fact, over the years our family had the blessing of having others live with us for extended periods of time and felt that we were able to "adopt" family members through hospitality and love.

As we researched the adoption process, we were shocked to find that the waiting list for a healthy American baby was five years long! We didn't want to wait that long, so we decided to look into international adoption. We went through Holt International, a wonderful Christian adoption agency, and within two year's time we were blessed to receive the news that we could adopt our son, Jabok Kang, from Seoul, Korea. We would later name him Joshua Philip Jabok Fenlon.

International adoption was not without its challenges. Mostly because we were the first family to adopt an international child in our county in Northern Michigan and no one really knew what the procedures entailed. Fortunately, my lovely wife did a lot of research and pushed the process along, educating our county officials, sometimes much to their chagrin, along the way.

Joshua was born on March 11, 1975, however he was thirteen

months old when he arrived here in the U.S.A. I remember we drove to Chicago to pick him at O'Hare International airport. What an experience! We were a bit nervous but extremely excited at the same time. On top of that we had never driven in Chicago before and I think I swore never to come back again if we got out of there alive. We were kidding of course, but I was very nervous driving in that much traffic! It was an experience for sure, and we did a lot of praying for safety.

So now our family had a new member! Joshua was a happy, loving little boy and he fit right in. He was all boy and loved sports even at a young age. I remember the adoption agency had also given us advice on what to feed Josh until he was acclimated to our America way of eating. Well, Josh jumped right in, he loved food, all kinds of it. Joshua was instantly a part of our family and we did not even think of him as being adopted. He was *our son* and Sarah's little brother.

By 1977 Susan and I felt like our family was not complete yet and we decided to look into adopting again. To our surprise the wait list for adopting a healthy American baby was even longer this time, ten years! At that point they were no longer even taking names for their wait list. So we decided to pursue international adoption once again. Before we were able to begin that process we found out that Susan was pregnant.

I remember the doctors wanted us to do testing to see if the baby Susan was carrying had any birth defects. I guess they wanted to do the tests so that they could give us options in the event our child had any birth defects. We decided there was no reason to do any testing. What difference would it make? We knew we were going to have this baby and love him/her no matter what. So we prayed, as we

always did on a regular basis, and asked God for a healthy
baby and a safe delivery.

On July 17, 1978, we welcomed Jacob Aldrich Fenlon into
our family. This pregnancy went a lot smoother than the
first one. Jacob was a healthy baby boy with all his fingers
and toes and no sign of the birth defect Sarah had been
born with! God is good! Because life isn't interesting enough
with two little kids and a baby, we decided we weren't done!
We now had two boys and only one girl. We truly felt God
was leading us to have one more child. The desire to adopt
was still on our hearts. So to complete our family we looked
to international adoption once again. We returned to Holt
International Adoption Agency to adopt from Seoul, Korea.
Our baby girl, Yung Jo Kim, was born July 19, 1980! We
would later name her Rebekah Lillian Yung Jo Fenlon. She
was six months old when she arrived. This time we got to
pick our baby up in Detroit. This airport was a bit closer and
easier to get to than our last experience at O'Hare
International airport in Chicago. I remember seeing
Rebekah for the first time. She was so tiny! She was six
months old yet was in newborn diapers. However, it didn't
take long for Rebekah to discover her love of American food
and to acclimate to life here. In our hearts and minds she
was a part of the Fenlon family even before she arrived!

I remember whenever we would go out to restaurants,
picnics, sightseeing, etc., many times people would ask us
about our adopted children. We would comment to each
other later, when this would happen we would have to think
about what they were asking us because we didn't view our
children as adopted. They were just our kids, period.

**What is unique about the way God put your family
together? Thank Him for it!**

ROCK PILES

I n the Old Testament of the Bible, many times when the Israelites had an encounter with God, they would build a memorial, a pile of rocks. They would do so knowing that if they passed that way again, they would remember what God had done for them there in that place.

I thought that it was a really cool idea. So, in my mind whenever God has done something in my life, I metaphorically see a pile of rocks. I have many rock piles in my life and this book is full of them. Probably because I'm so old! But mostly because God is so good! (If there's anything you get from this book, I hope it is the realization that God is good!) I'd like to share a couple of specific memories, some of those rock piles, with you in this chapter.

One of the first big rock piles I laid down came about when I was working on my car one day. The car was an old Rambler American. I was *constantly* having trouble with the carbure-

tor. This particular day Susan was working, I believe at a
Sears store, and I was home with Sarah and Joshua. I started
to work on the carburetor again because the car didn't want
to *stay* running. I had pulled the carburetor apart with the
car parked in the yard without anything underneath it
except grass. As I pulled the needle valve out, the spring that
holds the valve in place fell onto the ground. For those who
may have never had the occasion to pull apart a carburetor,
you may not understand the problem here: you cannot run
the car without that spring holding the needle valve in
place! I looked frantically for that spring for what seemed
like hours though it was probably only fifteen minutes or so.
It *seemed* like an eternity, and I could not find that spring. I
pushed the car back for several feet and then had Joshua
and Sarah, who were probably three and four at the time,
help me look for the spring. After another fifteen or twenty
minutes, I *resorted* to prayer. I know, I know. I should have
prayed over a half an hour earlier, but I was too frustrated to
think straight! Anyway, I finally asked for divine interven-
tion because I needed to pick Susan up from work and I
needed the car to run. I remember as my head rested on the
front fender of that old Rambler, I asked God to help me
find the spring. I specifically asked Him to let that spring be
between my feet when I opened my eyes. And do you know
what I saw when I opened my eyes? With my head still on
the fender, I looked and there between my feet was the
needle valve spring. WOW! That was so cool! There is no
way that spring should have been where I found it. It had
fallen on the ground several feet from where it was found,
where God had placed it for me to find. I will never forget
that experience.

· · ·

Another major rock pile was placed around the same time in my life. It was in the 70's. For whatever reason, at that time I had started to have migraine headaches as well as panic attacks. I struggled with them for at least two years on a fairly consistent basis. I distinctly remember that my migraines seemed to come at the most inopportune times. They were so severe I couldn't function. I had to lie down, have a cold cloth over my eyes, in as dark a room as possible, with NO NOISE. It was terrible. And the panic attacks... the panic attacks were scary! I remember the first time I had one I thought I was having a heart attack. I was in my early twenties at the time and was extremely healthy otherwise. I played softball and basketball and worked hard at the Proctor and Gamble factory in Cheboygan.

I couldn't understand why I was having these health issues. So, I went to God. I know, again, why didn't I do that sooner? I probably did *mention* it to Him once or twice before but did not talk about it to the extent that I did one day. I finally took time to really spend with God asking Him about the migraines and the panic attacks. I was to the point where I *had to* have an answer and I was going to keep taking it to God until I got one. Again, God spoke to me. And again, I can't explain what that sounded like or if it was even audible. All I know is that I was sure God heard me crying out to Him. He said to me, "Gary, do you trust Me?"

I've found that usually when God speaks, at least to me, it's in the form of a question.

"Of course," I answered, "Yes, Father, I do trust You!"

He answered me by simply saying, "Then give it all to Me."

.   .   .

In that moment the light came on and I suddenly realized I was doing *so many* things that were good things, but not things I had asked God about. I was a volunteer on several committees, I was playing sports, I was working hard and I was trying to spend time with my wife and kids. In short, I had just spread myself too thin, and my body was letting me know that I was pushing myself too hard and taking things too seriously.

The first thing I did was to ask God what He wanted me to be doing that would allow me to be a good example as a Christian both for my family as well as for my community. As I prayed, the Holy Spirit led me to slow down, change some of my schedule, get off some committees and spend more time in communion with God. It was at this time that I started to really learn what it was to be what I call "God-conscious". I know that God is omnipresent (He's always everywhere), and thereby He is with me every second of everyday. I started to talk with Him like I would a best friend. Many times, if I was working on a car, doing chores, hauling firewood, painting, driving, etc., I would talk with Him because I knew He was literally right next to me.

As I made the necessary changes in how I spent my time, I started to give more and more of my life and everything in it to my heavenly Father. It was something I needed to do (we all do) but it was a process. It didn't happen overnight. The Bible tells us in Philippians 4:6-7: "Do not be anxious about anything, but in every situation, by prayer and petition, with thanksgiving, present your requests to God. And the peace of God, which transcends all understanding, will guard your hearts and minds in Christ Jesus." It didn't take me very long to realize how much more relaxed I was, I was experiencing this peace that Paul wrote about in Philippians. And then it dawned on me. Since that time that God had spoken to me and I had made some immediate changes, including giving things to Him, I had not had another migraine or panic attack, nor have I had one since! As I write this I realize that was over forty years ago. God is extraordinarily good!

Soon after God healed me from my migraines and panic attacks He began teaching me to trust in Him more and more. During one of these "trust exercises" I was asked by the pastor of St. Thomas Lutheran Church, Pastor Mantei, to lead an adult Bible study on Sunday mornings before the church service. By this time, Susan and I had led the youth group at St. Thomas for several years and during that time I had many conversations with Pastor Mantei about the Bible and theology in general. So I imagined that through our conversations he must have been impressed with my knowledge of the Bible.

However, even though I had been invited to lead the study, I still battled with low self-esteem, and I did not like speaking in public or having to lead anything. As I sought God about this opportunity as to whether or not it was something I should do, I knew that God was calling me to it. So, I said yes. I remember my first Sunday morning leading this Bible study, which the pastor sat in on. My voice was cracking and I believe my knees were knocking together under the table I was so nervous. But I did it. No panic attack, no migraine.

Because there is a difference between feeling nervous about doing something out of obedience to the will of God and doing a bunch of things you think you should do because it might please Him or others. I taught the class because I wanted to be obedient to what I knew God was asking me to do, even if I didn't like it. In return He gave me the strength to do it even when I felt like I *couldn't*. Another rock pile.

Is there a time in your life that you can remember where you would build a rock pile, a place and time to remember the good that God has done in your life?

11

A CHRISTIAN SCHOOL

F or the next few years we focused on raising our family. I love sports and was able to play basketball and softball during that time as well. I had started work at UPS and Susan worked a few jobs here and there and took care of the kids and our home. It was in the late 70's that God led us to send our kids to a Christian school. We initially sent our first two children to North Central Christian Academy in Burt Lake, Michigan, which was a forty-minute bus ride one way.

God began to speak to my heart about starting a Christian school in Cheboygan. This turned out to be a huge rock pile for me, as God had to do so many things to make that school a reality. I took the idea to the pastor of our church and he told me to take it to the church board, which I did. Next, I was told to take the pulse of the church body on the subject. So I polled the entire congregation. With the exception of a couple of public school teachers, the response was over-whelmingly positive. The next step was to get authorization from the hierarchy in the Lutheran district that our church belonged to. We presented the idea to the board and they were also highly in favor of the endeavor to the degree that they were willing to give us $10,000 to help with the start up costs of the school.

It looked like everything was falling into place quite smoothly. The church was behind it and offered their educational wing with classrooms complete with desks and chalkboards. We were even going to have money to buy books or anything else needed to get going. I was very pleased with how it was going forward and I remember thinking, "Wow God, you are really opening the doors."

All of a sudden, things took a turn. Our church was in the process of hiring an associate pastor. A young man freshly out of seminary was called to be the associate pastor. The problem was, from the first day he arrived, he was very much against starting a Christian School in the church. I tried reasoning with him and tried to find out why he was so against having the school. All he said to me was that he didn't believe the church could afford to start a school and pay two pastors as well. I was really confused and asked God, "What is going on here?" Everything seemed perfect until this new pastor came onto the scene.

Well, I realized shortly thereafter that our family would not be staying at that church. We found we could not sit under the teaching of the new pastor. I will not get into details here, let me just say: I tried. I met with this pastor numerous times to discuss the bible and theology for hours. In the end we simply could not agree on some of the basics of biblical teaching and therefore I could not in good faith keep my family in the church.

I have to admit it was at this point I began questioning God. Why was this happening? What about the Christian school? Had I missed His will on this? Did I misunderstand what I had heard? Despite the questions in my heart I felt peace in leaving the church and knew God would show me what to do with this desire for a Christian school. For a short time we were checking out other churches as well as doing "church" on our own. But the desire for starting a Christian school did not go away. So I felt God was telling me to get the word out to the Christian community and see where it would go from there. And that's what I did. To my pleasant surprise, at our first meeting we had approximately fifteen to twenty men and women show up. From that group about ten or twelve really felt a Christian school was something that our community needed. I had prayed for people that could fill in the gaps in areas that I was not very good at. God was faithful to raise up a group of people that were very well rounded and knew how to keep the ball rolling as we started this adventure.

Our school, Cornerstone Christian School, spent its first year at the Evangelical Covenant Church, which was very much on board with what we wanted to do. The only problem was that our enrollment had a cap on it due to the zoning commission. Even though it had a newer facility, the church was not built to specifications to properly house a school. And to meet the requirements it would have cost tens of thousands of dollars. We went into it knowing this would be a short-term stay at the church for our school, but we had a school. We rested in knowing that God was fulfilling the vision for a a Christian school in Cheboygan. God would later provide land that would house our school and everything else we needed in between. I saw God bring into being what He had spoken to my heart those many years ago.

Do you have a vision or a dream, words that God may have spoken to you? Do you wonder how it will come about or if you will ever see its fulfillment? Have you sought God about it?

12

ANOTHER CHURCH

L et me start by saying, I don't think anyone, including myself, should leave a church unless you are sure God is leading you out. I/we prayed long and hard before we felt God had led us out of the church we had been attending. In Susan's case it was the only church she had ever known. So it was not a move made quickly nor was it a move that was easy to make. However we both really felt the peace of God in leaving. I also say when you are facing any major decision in your life, lift it up in prayer, then follow the path of peace. If you are listening to the Holy Spirit's leading, He will always lead you down a path of peace.

As a UPS driver one of my areas of delivery was the Harbor Springs area. It was here that I made deliveries to a church called Harbor Light Chapel, pastored by Bill Mindel. I was impressed with the people I met as I delivered there and especially was impressed with Pastor Bill.

To make a long story shorter, we visited the church and immediately felt that peace I had mentioned. Susan and I both felt that God was indeed leading us to attend Harbor

Light Chapel. I have to say it was a great time of learning while we attended there. Pastor Bill and the eldership there were wonderful Christian leaders. They also had a Christian school and I had hoped that I might learn some important lessons from them in how to run our school in Cheboygan. Then, much to my surprise, one of the elders and his wife at Harbor Light, who had been instrumental in starting their school, offered to help us with our new school endeavor.

The school was outgrowing the portable classrooms we were using and negotiated a deal with the U.S. Coast Guard for some property on Western Avenue where a facility approximately 40 ft. by 60 ft. was erected. That school, Cornerstone Christian School, is still there today. We managed to send our four kids through that school. Financially it was tough but somehow God made a way. God is faithful and He is good.

I am still amazed that God would give me, an ordinary guy, this kind of vision and that it would come to pass. When I say I'm an ordinary guy, I mean I do not have any degrees, college education or any special training. That being said I'm special because I am a child of God, but as a child of God you are very special too. When I think of God using me for His purposes, I think of how God used people in the Bible. Most of them were just like me, the ones most people would be surprised that God would choose to do things for Him. I think of 1 Corinthians 1:26-29. It says: "Brothers think of what you were when you were called. Not many of you were wise by human standards; not many were influential; not many were of noble birth. But God chose the foolish things of the world to shame the wise; God chose the weak things of the world to shame the strong. He chose the lowly things of this world and the despised things-and the things that are not-to nullify the things that are, so that no one may boast before Him."

When I read that passage I especially think of the biblical accounts of David and Golaith and Gideon. God chose a teen boy to take down a giant. He chose a man who considered himself to be the least of the least and yet used him to accomplish His will. So the point is, yes God can and usually does, use ordinary people to accomplish extraordinary things.

An interesting aspect of the nucleus of people that started Cornerstone Christian School is that we were a group of ordinary individuals seeking the will of an extraordinary God. There were doctors, lawyers, contractors and other people with impressive skills and knowledge, but we were all being obedient to what we felt God was calling us to do. At that time many of them were in between churches as well. Many started attending Harbor Light Chapel along with my family. Before we knew it, we had several families from Cheboygan attending there. I remember some of the Harbor Light parishioners had helped us with various aspects of expanding Cornerstone Christian School. From this group of people and with the help of Harbor Light Chapel, a new church in Cheboygan arose called Cornerstone Chapel. After some time, Cornerstone Chapel would be renamed River of Life Church.

The name change came about mostly because many people had a hard time separating the school from the church since they both had the same name. Also the school was to be run by an independent board, open to all Christians in our community and not run by Cornerstone Chapel alone. Thus, the name change.

Have you asked God where He wants you to be?

13

COACHING MEMORIES

One of my favorite things that God had me get involved in was coaching soccer. First, let me say I didn't and still don't like soccer much (sorry, to you soccer fans). Second, I knew NOTHING about soccer. A coach was needed for summer league junior high age boys and girls and since some of my kids were playing, I agreed to help out.

The first thing I did was to get a book on basic soccer. I didn't even know the names of the positions, let alone any strategy. As I prayed about coaching the kids, which I believed God wanted me to do, one of the first thoughts that came to mind was to make sure the kids had fun. Again, I believe we live in a time where kids are not allowed to just be kids. I also wanted to impart to the them the importance of playing as a team, respecting themselves and their team-mates, as well as their opponent. If we accomplished those goals then we would have a successful season regardless of wins and losses.

. . .

I coached about seven years and we had a lot of fun. The teams I coached were usually very successful. One of the times I will never forget came in one of the first years I coached. I had a young girl who had a really low self-esteem and was a bit on the heavy side. She was an introvert and very quiet. I knew she had come from a divorced home situation and just sensed that she needed some fun and something good to happen in her life. So I tried everything I could think of to her help feel better about herself. Of course, I tried that with all of the kids, but this girl seemed to really need it.

As the story goes I always nicknamed the kids different names depending on their talents. Names like Wolfman (it could be a boy or girl), Head-hunter, Flash, Lightning, Go-getter, etc. Well this girl in particular couldn't run very fast, but boy could she kick a soccer ball. She could kick it further than anyone on our team. I nicknamed her Thunderfoot. We had a great season. As memory serves me, we were undefeated and we were playing another undefeated team for the championship. Our opponent scored first and led 1 to 0. Their coach decided to do what is called pack the box (the area in front of the goal). He did this so we couldn't dribble the ball anywhere close to their goal. He intended on winning the game 1 to 0. So at half time I devised a plan. I won't say I prayed for wisdom, but I have got to say God definitely helped. The plan was to drive the ball as far as possible toward the opponent's goal then to kick the ball back to Thunderfoot. I told Thunderfoot to kick the ball at the goal since she could kick the ball the furthest of any of our players. The idea was, if we can't go through the traffic in front of the goal, then we would go over it.

To my amazement, that girl, Thunderfoot, kicked in two goals that were perfectly placed between the crossbar and the goalie's outstretched arms, and we won the championship game. Those were the only two goals that Thunderfoot had scored all year, but she was the star of the game. I remember watching those two shots go into the net and it was like I was watching it in slow motion. I truly believe somehow God directed those two shots perfectly. Now, I didn't pray to win, but I always prayed we would do our best and have fun doing it. I remember the next year Thunderfoot's mother came to me and asked if she could play for me again. I told her I don't pick the teams and only coach whomever they assign to me. She told me that game changed her daughter's life. She came out of her shell, gained some self-confidence, and started to feel good about herself. I do know that Thunderfoot started working out and went on to be a high school star in soccer and in volleyball. God is good!

What is God calling you to do that you feel ill equipped to do?

Can you imagine what God can do for you and others if you will only obey?

14

FAMILY CHALLENGES

One of the first major challenges in the life of our family occurred in July 1984. This was when Susan's mother, Mildred, passed away after having a heart attack at the age of 59. Of course we had been praying for her and it was difficult to understand why God had not healed her. She was a woman of great faith and her healing took place in heaven, not on this earth.

Isaiah 55:8-9 says, "For my thoughts are not your thoughts neither are your ways my ways declares the Lord. As the heavens are higher than the earth, so are my ways higher than your ways and my thoughts than your thoughts."

Her mother's death caught Susan so much off guard that she went into a depression that without the grace of God could have destroyed our marriage. This depression lasted for what seemed to be forever, but in reality it was a bit over two years, which is still a long time. During this time she struggled to just get out of bed let alone do much with the kids or me.

.   .   .

It was also during this time as our marriage struggled that I was seemingly tempted to be unfaithful every other day. I don't ever recall having so many women hit on me. I suddenly realized that the enemy, Satan, knew where our marriage was the most vulnerable. I do remember crying out to God to do something time and time again. After two years I finally told God, while literally on my knees, that I could not handle it anymore. It was shortly after that God pulled Susan out of it. God is good even though His timing is not our timing. And even though I would never want to go through that again, I know that there is a purpose in the things that happen to us. I also know that God uses these times of testing to purify and strengthen our faith. 1 Peter 1:6-7: "In this you rejoice, though now for a little while, if necessary, you have been grieved by various trials, so that the tested genuineness of your faith - more precious than gold that perishes though it is tested by fire - may be found to result in praise and glory and honor in the revelation of Jesus Christ."

Are you in the midst of a trial? Can you see a revelation of Jesus Christ your Savior in the midst of your trouble?

15

MAJOR CHALLENGES

The next huge challenge in our family came a few years later. It's what I at times refer to as the year from hell. I'm not even sure where to start here. Some of what I'm going to write seems like a dream, mostly a bad dream at that. Some of the memories are clouded and hard to remember clearly. I think some of them I just truly don't want to remember. However, I will do my best to share what I remember from my perspective, so here we go: It was in the summer of 1991 and our first born Sarah was diagnosed with bone cancer (osteogenic sarcoma) just before her senior year of high school at Cheboygan Area Schools.

Sarah had been a cheerleader, played soccer and she ran track. Shortly after she was diagnosed we went to Mayo Clinic in Rochester Minnesota for a second opinion. I remember when we found out it was definitely bone cancer. I also remember telling Sarah, after she came out of recovery from her biopsy, that she had a tumor and she would need surgery to remove the cancer. After we had a good cry together, she said something I will never forget.

She said to me, "Dad, I'm glad it's me and not another family member. I will be ok. God will get me through this."

I could not have been more proud of her. As time went on and she had surgeries, to have her knee removed and replaced, she kept that positive spirit. Her doctors and nurses told us that they were impressed with her fighting spirit. They said that attitude is half the battle to successfully beating cancer.

After the biopsy, Sarah, for almost a year, had to go Motts Children's Hospital in Ann Arbor, Michigan for chemotherapy treatment. There were also trips back to Mayo Clinic for surgeries intermingled during that year. Over the course of these months, after some of the chemo to shrink the tumor, Sarah returned, on her 18th birthday, to Mayo Clinic to have surgery and a knee replacement.

Yet God was so faithful. For example, on one of the trips I took to Mayo Clinic to visit Susan and Sarah out there, I had asked my boss at UPS if I could get done as early as possible on a Friday to travel to Mayo Clinic for the weekend for a visit. He said it would be no problem and he made sure I had as light a delivery day as possible. That afternoon I finished my route and returned to the UPS Center. As I prepared to drive my older vehicle to Minnesota, my boss told me to take his brand new van instead of my old car. He also told me it was full of gas and to bring it back on empty.

I also need to mention how our church and our community of Cheboygan stepped up to help us during this difficult time for our family. There were donations made and different fundraisers held that were for our benefit. I/we will never forget the outpouring of good wishes, support, prayers, and the generosity of our small community.

Without their help, a difficult situation would have been much worse.

Another blessing occurred a short time later when a family from a local church donated their newer mini-van to that church, and it was offered to our family to use for as long as we needed it. My wife and I no longer had to drive our old car to either Ann Arbor or to Mayo Clinic. Over the course of almost a year with that van we managed to put over 50,000 miles on it.

Again, God was faithful. During those 50,000 plus miles in less than a year Sarah and her mother never got lost in their travels and that van never had a flat tire, never broke down, never left them stranded during their travels. Remember this was a time before cell phones, on-star and navigation systems!

Yes, God was faithful. I especially remember one trip Rebekah and I took to visit Saran and Susan at the Mayo Clinic. We travelled in the middle of winter and during a major snowstorm. We had to follow a snowplow across Wisconsin because the snow was so deep. When we got to Minnesota, the roadway was a sheet of ice. There were numerous accidents and vehicles in the ditches, yet that van made it through without missing a beat. I was amazed at how well it handled and got us through deep snow and then across icy roads. Praise God.

Sarah missed most of her senior year of high school. But she wanted to graduate with her class, so she did most of her homework from home and kept her grades up so she could graduate come May 1992, and she did with honors.

The monthly routine included the following: after church on Sunday, going to the local hospital, having blood work done to determine where Sarah's blood counts were, then if the counts were good enough Sarah and Susan

would head off to Ann Arbor Sunday afternoon to be at the
hospital for early Monday morning to start treatment. This
went on for three weeks and then they would get two weeks
off at home to recover a bit from the effects of the chemo
before starting the monthly routine over again.

It was in the middle of Sarah's treatment that Susan's
father, Chancey, was diagnosed with lung cancer and given
a few months to live. Also during this time period I had
been injured working at UPS and I missed almost six
months of work. Yes, there were many challenges we were
facing.

Yet one of the blessings during this time occurred when
Sarah won a contest at University of Michigan Mott's Children's Hospital. She won an all-expenses paid trip for two to
the Men's Basketball Final Four weekend in Minnesota. I'm
a huge basketball fan and my favorite college team,
Michigan (GO BLUE), was in the finals that year. For U of M
basketball fans, this was the fab-five era! So not only did
Sarah and I get an all-expenses paid trip to the finals, but
our team was in it! God is good!

Another blessing for our family was Sarah's attitude. She
is such a fighter. She hardly ever complained, at least not
that I can remember. She took this cancer head on. I
remember because she was still 17, she was placed in the
pediatric ward at Mott's Children's Hospital in Ann Arbor.
Since she had such a positive attitude the nurses would
bring in the new patients to visit with her. She was always
an encouragement to the other kids. I remember one time
when I was with her, (most of the time I did not make the
trip, either I was working when able, or staying with our
other children) as I walked into her room there in bed with
her was a small girl about seven years old and Sarah was
reading a book to her. Sarah's faith and fight were truly

inspirational. Yet it was difficult. At that time cancer was winning most of the battles. As I remember in less than one year, of about twenty kids that came through the same time as Sarah, only six made it through. The rest died from their disease. Each death brought about sorrow for everyone who had met them.

When Chancey was nearing the end of his life, we were wondering how we were going to get Sarah to Ann Arbor for chemo and yet be there for Chancey. As we prayed I had a sense that somehow God would work out the details. On this particular Sunday after church we took Sarah to the local Cheboygan hospital for blood work to prepare to travel to Ann Arbor. I remember the E.R. doctor kind of freaking out that Sarah's blood counts were so low and not where they needed to be. I immediately called her oncologist in Ann Arbor and handed the phone to the E. R. doctor. The oncologist told the E. R. doctor what to do for Sarah and they told us to not come that week to Ann Arbor. Out of all the treatment and chemotherapy that year, this would be the only week Sarah's blood counts were not good enough to go through chemo. That week we were all home and that week Susan's father died.

I believe that it was God who had His hand in the timing of it all. Just about three months before Chancey died he had asked Jesus to be Lord of his life. That made his passing so much easier to bear for those of us who loved him. Life can be difficult to navigate with God, but without Him, I can't even imagine how people get through.

What challenges are you facing today? How is God proving Himself to be faithful even in the midst of those things that might feel the most difficult?

16

MORE CHALLENGES

All that I relayed in the last chapter sets the stage for another huge challenge we were about to face. As I stated earlier, I had been injured and could not work for approximately six months. During that time we had a couple of weeks where *everything* went wrong for us. We were out at Mayo clinic and as we returned home we found out our son Joshua had gotten our old car stuck in the snow. When he had tried to get it out of the snow he trashed the motor. After that, within the course of just a few days our oven broke, our dryer broke, the drain field in our back yard quit working (meaning we couldn't flush the toilet), then our pump burned up on our well and we couldn't get any water. On top of that we were facing bankruptcy. From all the travel, motel rooms, doctor bills, food, gas, etc. we were severely in debt. I had good credit and I ran up every credit card I could get to keep the family financially afloat. We were close to $50,000 in debt. But we had come to the end of trying to pay our bills. And it seemed impossible to even *attempt to find a way* to fix some of the necessities in our home.

. . .

I did not know what more to do. As I confided in some close friends and prayer partners, they asked me if I was caught up in some type of sin. I told them I was not. Honestly, I felt a bit like Job in the Bible. Even my friends thought I must have something wrong in my life.

The turning point came on a beautiful, clear, cold winter's night. I couldn't sleep and did not know what to do. It was one o'clock in the morning and I went outside, knelt down in a snow bank and cried out to God. I wasn't angry, but I was at the end of what I knew to do. I asked God what I might have done to deserve what was going on in my life. I felt like the weight of the world was on my shoulders and I could not carry it anymore. Once again, God spoke to me. Again, I cannot explain it but I could hear God's voice.

He said to me, "Gary, do you trust Me?"

I replied, "Yes, Sir, I do. I've got nowhere else to go."

Then He said to me, "Then give it all to Me!"

That was the extent of our conversation. So, I started with Sarah.

I said, "Father if she lives or dies I will still follow You. I want her to live..."

Then I gave Him my wife and the rest of our kids. After that I gave up our home and any and all possessions. I gave Him everything.

In a sense, I laid everyone, everything on the altar. It made me think of an account in Genesis 22. The Bible tells us of the testing of Abraham. God told Abraham to place his son

Isaac on an altar. I love this passage of scripture, where (to my knowledge) it is the first time we find three particular words used in the Bible. Those words are: testing, love and worship. Because of those words I believe this is a pivotal chapter. The fact that those words are used together lays the groundwork for our lives. At my point of *testing*, I theoretically laid everything I *loved* on the altar and told God the most important thing in my life at this point was my relationship with Him and I would *worship* and follow Him no matter the results. In Matthew 22:37, Jesus said this is the most important thing we can do: to love God above everything else. Jesus also said in Matthew 10:39: "Whoever finds his life will lose it, and whoever loses his life for my sake will find it." Jesus is talking about total surrender to Him. Giving Him our lives. That's not always easy and it's truly a daily challenge. But this I know - whatever I have truly surrendered to God, He has more often than not given back in abundance.

As I gave up everything, I literally felt like a hundred-pound weight had been lifted off of my shoulders. I went to bed and for the first time in weeks and slept like a baby. I woke up the next morning and as I was looking into the mirror to shave, I realized I was smiling. I hadn't smiled in quite some time due to the stress of it all. But there it was: a smile! I had what the Bible in Philippians 4:7 calls "the peace that passes all understanding." I must say whenever I'm facing tough times, I always go back to that rock pile of kneeling in that snowbank and hearing the voice of God. I will never forget God meeting me there, and I will never forget that peace that truly passes all human understanding. It was supernatural. Nothing about our circumstances had seemingly changed, but *I* had changed. Our God is good and He is faithful to hear our cry and free us of our burdens if we will let Him.

Will you surrender your burdens to Him and allow Him to work in your life?

17

GOD IS ALWAYS GOOD

I had some friends of mine tell me I should file for bankruptcy, but after praying about it and talking it over with Susan, I really felt God was telling me not to do that. I'm so thankful for a supportive wife. After discussing with her about our financial mess, Susan basically told me she would support whatever decision I made. I felt God had told me to work my way out of debt, so that's what I decided to do.

In a short time I received a couple of phone calls, one was from a family friend who said he would come out and put in a new drain field for us and I could pay him later. The other call was from another family we knew, who were well drillers, and they said they had a used water pump that they would install and I could pay them later. So two major necessities were taken care of within a few days.

Next I spoke with our local mortgage lender and they

granted me a bit more time to catch up on our house payments.

I was amazed once again how God showed up in our time of need. God is always faithful even when we are not. He is faithful even when things don't go the way we want them to. One of the first scriptures I memorized as a Christian was Romans 8:28: "And we know that in all things God works for the good of those who love Him who have been called according to His purpose."

I believe this scripture with my whole heart because I've seen God's hand at work throughout my life even and especially in times of struggle and heartache. That passage *does not* say everything in our lives will be good, but rather that God in His infinite wisdom will bring good out of the circumstances in our lives. Even if we cannot see it immediately or even perhaps never in our lifetime, God's goodness is always there.

When I say that, I think of my mother-in-law, Millie. She prayed for her husband, my father-in-law, Chancey, all of her life. She prayed that he would come to know Jesus until the day she died. I know this because she would, from time to time, ask me to keep praying along with her. In this life she never saw the fruit of those prayers. However, in the end, just months before his death, Chancey asked Jesus to be His Lord. Now I know that they are celebrating in heaven together.

. . .

God is always good, even and maybe especially, when we can't see our way out of our mess. Our financial mess did not go away quickly. It took consistent and faithful efforts on our part. Those steps added up to over twenty years before we finally achieved our goal of being credit card debt free. Often, we want the quick fix however situations don't always resolve in our timeline and we must rely on our faith in a good God to see the results we desire.

Is there an area of your life that you feel is bankrupt? Remember Romans 8:28. Will you trust God to work things for your good?

18

MOVING FORWARD

By the grace of God, we made it through that long year from July 1991 when Sarah was first diagnosed with bone cancer until June 2, 1992, the day of her last chemo. She ended up graduating with her class that year. I will never forget that day. I was so proud of my little girl. As she walked across the stage to accept her diploma she received a standing ovation from the hundreds of parents, friends and families in attendance that day. Even one of Sarah's doctors from the University of Michigan hospitals came to witness her graduation. What an awesome young woman. God is good.

Sarah started community college and our oldest son Joshua graduated from high school in 1993. He joined the Marines right after and soon we were driving him down-state to see him off for boot camp. It was emotional, letting Josh go into the military. We tried to get back to a normal life-routine, including me being healthy enough to get back to work. I had begun working around fifty hours a week for UPS again and I was looking for ways to make extra money outside of that job as well.

A few months earlier, I had been playing basketball (no, I cannot dunk, even though I dream about it!) with one of my teammates who was the local recruiter for the Michigan Army National Guard. He knew about the financial struggles our family was facing and he suggested I consider getting back into the Guard. I did think about it. After much discussion with Susan and much prayer, I/we decided to give it a try. So, in March of 1993 I rejoined the National Guard.

I worked for UPS for 31 years and I have many memories of that time. Some great, some not so great, but I thanked God for a good steady job. UPS provided for my family and I for all of those years.

One of the most vivid memories I have from UPS is of one clear, winter day, around the third week of March in the early nineties. I was hurrying to complete my day of deliveries. I was in a rush because it was a Friday and our son Jacob was playing in a hockey tournament downstate. Susan had already departed with the mom of one of Jacob's teammates and had taken the kids down earlier in the day. I was to meet up with the teammate's father and we were to ride together to the tournament after work. I was trying to finish my route as early as possible as a result of these plans. It was a beautiful, sunny day with dry roads. I had almost completed my route for the day and was heading west on a two-lane paved road that headed towards a large lake called Mullett Lake in Northern Michigan. As I approached a point in the road where I needed to make a left turn I stepped on my brakes and to my surprise realized I had none. I quickly asked Jesus for help. The paved road was bare and I was probably travelling around 55 mph. This road eventually came to a T, the paved road going to my left at a 90 degree angle and a dirt road going to the right at a 90 degree angle. The third option was to go straight down a small hill to where another dirt road stopped at the lake. I quickly realized I was going too fast to turn either to the right or to the left. I knew I would probably roll the truck over if I tried making either of those turns. Next, I tried pulling on the emergency brake and it did nothing. I decided I had to go straight ahead down the small hill toward the lake. I tried to down shift the truck (it was a manual 4-speed transmission), as I went flying through the intersection of the turns I could not make, I got the truck to downshift into a lower gear to try and slow down. The rear tires locked up and made a screeching sound on the pavement. As the tires hit the dirt road the truck started to fishtail, still headed down the small hill toward the lake. At the end of the road there was a snowbank approximately two and a half to three feet high with a sign in the middle of it stating the road had ended. There was nothing but trees on either side of the road. I only had a couple of seconds to decide my fate. Should I take the truck into the trees? Should I jump out of the moving (too fast) truck? Or should I take the chance and hit the snowbank and proceed out onto the lake in hopes that there was enough ice under the snow to hold the weight of the truck?

I choose the latter. I tried to miss the sign but as I hit the snowbank, the sign ripped off one of my side mirrors. The truck went airborne as it hit the hard snowbank. (It was literally like the Dukes of Hazard if anyone remembers that TV show!). The truck landed on the hard pack snow almost perfectly and I quickly turned the steering wheel to go along the lakeshore on top of the snow/ice and stay away from deeper water. I didn't even know if the pack snow/ice would hold the weight of the truck. As soon as the truck stopped I immediately jumped out and got away from it in case it should start to sink. It didn't, thank God.

I walked to a home up on top of the hill to see if anyone was home so I could use the phone. (This was before cell phones). As I told my boss what had happened, at first he did not believe that my UPS truck was now sitting out on the ice on Mullett Lake. He later commended me on being able to keep the damage to a minimum. I also later found out that the ice on the lake had been especially thick that year. There was approximately still 8-10 inches on the lake. Now this did not happen every year, some years the ice would have already melted by late March. Praise God that my brakes went out in the right year! For many years after that my fellow employees would razz me about trying to drive my UPS truck across Mullett Lake.

Our family life moved on from some of the tough times we had been going through. However, I/we soon found out that "normal family life" (whatever that is) was not going to happen like we would have liked. Life is full of changes. Change is not always easy, in fact most of the time it is hard. But change is inevitable. Change always happens, we cannot stop it. We age and our bodies change, people die and there are new lives brought into this world, there are job changes, and families move away, etc. Change is inevitable.

Is there a change coming in your life that you may be resisting? How can you make peace with the change that is to come? What do you need to let go of so that Jesus can take control?

19

A CALL TO PASTOR

I t happened one day in 1995. I don't remember exactly what I was doing, working on a car or maybe hauling firewood, but God spoke to me once again. He asked me a question, as He usually did and still does.

God said to me, "Do you know why you went through all of that in 1991 and 1992?"

"No, Sir," I answered.

God said, "It was to prepare you to be a pastor."

"I don't want to be a pastor," I said.

That was the extent of our conversation.

After much contemplation I began to think of Genesis 22 again, and realized that "the year from hell" was actually a test. A test that God allowed to see how I would handle it. I don't believe God sends bad things to us, but I do believe He knows what is coming our way. And God uses those difficult things we go through for our good and/or for the good of others.

. . .

Maybe it would be appropriate to take a moment here to explain the best that I can why bad things happen, even to good people. We live in a fallen world. It all started way back in Genesis chapter three when Adam and Eve, God's creation of mankind, decided to disobey God and do things their way. Yes, I know they were deceived by the serpent (Satan), but ultimately they had a choice. We all have choices. We either do things God's way or do things our way. Guess which way doesn't work? OUR WAY! In life our way hardly ever works out well. So, because of what is commonly known as "The Fall of Man", Adam and Eve's sin of disobedience, sin entered the world and has negatively affected all of creation ever since, and will continue to, until the return of Jesus Christ. Good people are sometimes hurt because of this Fall of Man, because of a sinful world.

I know that what I just wrote is probably an oversimplification, but I also know this: obedience to God typically results in blessings, and disobedience to the things of God usually results in pain.

So when God told me I would become a pastor I was not excited about that call on my life. I had worked closely with our previous pastors and I saw what they had to put up with, and to be honest I wanted no part of it. To be *completely* honest, I did not want the responsibility or the trouble of the office of pastor. But nonetheless, I also knew that I would do whatever God asked of me.

. . .

Have you ever asked yourself why bad things happen to good people? What has God spoken to your heart about this topic?

20

GRANDCHILDREN

Around this time in the life of our family, our youngest daughter, Rebekah, had become a teenager. As parents, Susan and I began to struggle with some of the behaviors that she began exhibiting.

It became clear that Rebekah did not want to be in our home. She would run away and sneaked out consistently. We tried talking with her, taking her to counseling and finally resorted to calling the police for her safety when she ran away. One of the hardest things we ever had to do was to turn her over to the court system. The choices she was making took control out of our hands. We felt helpless. As a parent you question yourself and wonder where you went wrong? How could your child be in so much turmoil? Was there something else you could have done? To this day I cannot answer those questions. I am blessed to be able to say that today we do have good relationships with all of our children.

. . .

Within a few years after leaving our home Rebekah was married and had two children, one boy and one girl. Those children, our first grandchildren, were rays of sunshine in our world! They were blessings in our lives. We enjoyed sharing "the country life" on our forty acres with them. We would explore, take walks in the woods, make birdhouses, pick flowers and soak in the hot tub together. It was pure joy spending time with them.

However, our grandchildren were taken from our lives when their parents split up. Their father took them to Texas and left us with no forwarding address or contact information. We were heart broken. There are no words to express the devastation we felt when those children were ripped from our lives. Oh, and by the way, in case you didn't already know or hadn't realized yet: life is NOT fair. That's where faith has to come in. In our brokenness, anger and despair all we can do is turn to God. We need Him to do what we cannot do, to heal our broken hearts and mend the pieces of our lives.

We very soon realized that we had to release our grandchildren into God's hands and to trust Him with their care. We constantly prayed for them but could not continue to dwell or focus on their absence from our lives. Focusing on our loss was not productive, so we began to lean into where God was leading us, the next phase of our lives.

. . .

Have you ever had a broken heart? Did you trust God with it? How did God heal you?

21

THE CALL FULFILLED

In August of 1998 I *still* wanted no part of being a pastor. I was one of the leaders, an elder, at River of Life Church. Our church attendance was falling. Our pastor was ready to move on and by the time he left the church, I was the only elder left. So I called a church meeting. At that time there were only about twenty members left.

I asked those in attendance what they wanted to do: should we close the church, continue on, or look for another pastor? General consensus was to continue on and look for another pastor. I was asked to lead the church until we found said pastor. I agreed. I knew I would need help. Fortunately, there were a few men I knew I could call on to do just that. There were three of them to be exact, two of whom were ex-pastors and one who was currently pastoring. They were all in the same church in Petoskey, Michigan just thirty miles away. These leaders offered to preach at our church two weeks a month and I would preach the other two. We also decided that once a month my wife Susan and I would meet with them to talk about how things were going at River of Life Church.

This went on for a few months. At one of our meetings with the three helpers, one of the men told me they felt that God was telling them I was supposed to pastor the church. They said I was preaching good sermons, making all the right decisions and handling the problems that arose with healthy solutions. I told them that I was not interested in pastoring the church, nor did I have the time.

I was still working for UPS as well as the National Guard doing drills one weekend a month and two weeks of summer camp every year. Along with preaching those two weeks a month and counseling when it was needed I was booked. I just didn't have time for what I thought would be proper training such as Bible College or even on-line bible courses. I was also heavily involved in jail ministry. About twice a week I was doing church services or bible studies at our local county jail. This was something I had been doing since about 1994. Put all of that together and I had very little down time.

The turning point came a couple of months later. Our daughter Sarah was getting her master's degree from Michigan State University in Lansing, Michigan and was attending Liberty Christian Church. Whenever we would visit her we would attend church with her. I quickly became friends with the pastor, Malcolm Magee. He and I would talk about my situation in leading River of Life Church until we could find a pastor, as well as theological issues. One day Malcolm called me and said something that set me back in my chair. He said he had been praying for River of Life and God had spoken to him during his time of prayer and told him that I was to be the pastor of the church. This was now the fourth pastor in a matter of a few months to give me the same message: I was to pastor River of Life Church. This was exactly what God had spoken to me about three years earlier. I finally, and yet reluctantly said "Okay, I give up, but God this is your church and I need a lot of help!" Thankfully, our church had several capable and Spirit-filled men who could help fill the pulpit, and I formed an eldership with these men.

I explained to Malcolm that I did not have time for Bible courses or specialized training. He told me that in the course of our conversations he had realized that God had given me the gift and the call to be a pastor. He saw in me things that I did not see (or feel).

He said, "Gary, you have what I call street-smarts. You've learned through experience and personal study. You don't need Bible College if you don't have time for it. In fact, I believe in you so much I'm willing to come up there and ordain you."

He gave me several theology books to study to help me further my education, and true to his word and conviction, on July 29, 2001, Malcolm ordained me as pastor of River of Life Church.

God is so good. I had been blessed to have the influence of several Godly men in my life. David LaHaie, while I was a young Christian, the late Bill Mindel from Harbor Light Chapel, Larry Staton, who was a former pastor (the first) of our church, Jim Larsen, now a retired pastor from Family of Christ Church, and of course, Malcolm Magee, the former pastor of Liberty Christian Church. There were many others over the years that I have not mentioned but God has always been faithful to surround me with those who will teach me and push me to stretch, grow and ultimately trust God for things that seem far beyond me.

Who can you call on to support you in God's call for your life? Who will speak the truth in love to you when you need to hear it?

22

SOME OF MY FAVORITE PASTOR-ISMS

There are a few sayings that I have always lived by. Here is one of them: Everyday is a good day just some are better than others. What I like about this statement is that we cannot always choose our circumstances, but we CAN choose how we *go through* our circumstances.

Another saying goes like this: If you spend your time doing the do's, you won't have time to do the don'ts. This is great because all we have to do is what we know is the right thing to do. When we are focused on what we need to do, we don't have time or energy for the *other* things. I know that sounds simple but I find so many people try to see how far they can go before they get burned, instead of staying away from the proverbial fire in the first place. James 4:17 says, "if anyone, then, knows the good they ought to do and doesn't do it, it is sin for them."

.   .   .

I've used both of these statements, as well as many others, in my lifetime of ministry. In the mid 90's God led me into jail/prison ministry. Through that work I pastor a lot of people who have made poor choices in life and are now facing the consequences of those choices. Doing the do's is extremely important, right? That can mean things like: staying away from some family members, changing friends, finding a different job and so on. It also should include going to church every time the doors are open, attending Bible studies, reading and studying the Bible on your own and hanging around people going the direction in life that you need/want to go. Developing new, healthy habits and doing those things I just mentioned is vital to seeing the changes you may want in your life.

It's really common sense but I'm always amazed at how many people just don't *see it*. Now, I don't want this to sound like a formula because, like I stated earlier, the Christian life is really all about relationship, first with God then with others. But this I know: if you do the right things you usually get right results. Of course then, the opposite is also true.

When people ask me questions about something going on in their lives, I ask them, "Well, what does the Bible say?" That by the way is *not* a cop out. The Bible really does have the answers to life's questions. I'm more interested in what God thinks about life rather than what Pastor Gary thinks. The Bible is a gold mine that never ends. It has one nugget of truth after another if only we will take the time to dig into it. 2 Timothy 3:16-17 says: "All scripture is God breathed, and is useful for teaching, rebuking, correcting and training in righteousness, so that the man (or woman) of God may be thoroughly equipped for every good work". That about covers it as far as to why we should study the Word of God and rely on it as a gauge and guide in our lives.

Another attribute I believe all Christians need today is the ability to hear the Holy Spirit. Jesus said many times, "he who has ears, let him hear." I'm sure almost everyone Jesus was talking about had ears, so whom was He referring to? I believe Jesus was telling us to use the ears we've been given, listen to the Holy Spirit and He will guide us. We as believers desperately need to be hearing and following the Holy Spirit in the age of distraction in which we live. There are so many competing voices in our culture today. Jesus told us in John 16:13 that the Holy Spirit would guide us into *all* truth. I pray for that guidance all the time. We need the Holy Spirit to empower us to do those do's and to convict us when we are tempted toward the don'ts.

What are some of your favorite -isms to live by?

Do they line up with the Word of God?

23

ALMOST DEAD AS A PASTOR

One of my many needs for guidance came during one experience when I didn't know what to do. I received a phone call a little after 1 AM. When you get a call at that time of night, you know it's usually not good. This particular call was about a man who I will call John (not his real name) whose wife attended River of Life on a fairly consistent basis. I had only met John a couple of times and ... let's just say: he was very interesting. He had been a former drug dealer and I had heard many stories of what his lifestyle had been before. The call that night was placed by a friend of John's. He told me that John and his wife had gotten into an argument and she had left him and he was contemplating hurting himself.

I got out of bed, got dressed and started praying for wisdom as I rushed down to their home. It was just before 2 AM on a warm summer's night when I arrived. The front door to their apartment was slightly ajar and when I knocked the door swung open. As I peered inside I saw that the television was on and across from the television next to the stairway to the second story sat two stuffed chairs. In the far chair John sat with the muzzle of a gun stuck in his mouth. As I was asking the Holy Spirit for wisdom and what to do, He answered me and said: "Do and say nothing". So I entered the home and sat down in the first stuffed chair and started watching (actually just looking in the direction of) the television.

As you can imagine one cannot talk with the muzzle of a gun stuck in the mouth. Eventually, John pulled the gun out of his mouth and looked at me and said, "What are you doing here?"

I answered, "Well, I got a phone call saying you might be about to do something stupid and I thought I had better get down here to talk with you before you did."

John proceeded to point the gun at me and said, "Well, I can kill you too!"

Now, what I'm about to tell you is something that was kind of strange. It totally took me by surprise and I'm not sure I can fully explain it, but here goes: As John was speaking to me I was thinking to myself, *Gary you should be scared!* But as I was looking down the barrel of a small rifle, I realized I was not scared at all. There was no fear whatsoever. I was actually amazed at what I was feeling. Then, out of nowhere, I heard myself say, "John, just do me a favor, if you shoot me, please kill me with the first shot!"

John responded, "You're crazy!"

I answered, "No I'm a wimp, I don't want to be crying out in pain, so kill me with the first shot if you are going to shoot me." Then I said: "I'm ready to die. I know where I will spend my eternity. But before you blow your brains all over the wall behind you, do you know where you are spending your eternity? If not then you had better give me that gun and we better talk."

So John did put down the gun and we did talk. Later that morning, I was able to pray with John that he would follow Jesus as Lord of his life. Soon after, he and his wife reconciled their differences and started attending church together. A few years later they moved downstate. We stayed in touch for a while and my wife and I even visited them one time when travelling through the town in which they lived. But as usually happens through the passage of time, we lost contact with each other.

Have you ever had a near-death experience? How did God show Himself faithful to you?

24

PREACHING SELF-WORTH

One truth is universal and I have seen it time and again in every area I have ever ministered: people struggle with self-worth. When people are hurting they often hurt others through words and actions. When we are hurt we have a choice. We can either turn to the truth of God and His Word or we can believe the words of others and falsely devalue ourselves. The enemy (the devil) also lies to people. He accuses them and causes them to believe they are worthless because of their faults and sins. They believe God could never forgive them, love them or use them for His purposes. These are lies that the devil uses all the time. Which leads me to ask: **What does the Bible say about you?** To answer that question I turned to the Word of God. I wanted to communicate to our church members their value and the depth of God's love for them. I wanted them to first confess then believe it. So, several years ago I started having everyone recite the following after me every Sunday: I am a gift from God. I am beautiful and of value. I am worthy to be loved. I am accepted by God. My life has meaning and purpose.

These are statements of truth as spoken by God in His Word. The more you confess something the deeper the seeds of truth are planted in your spirit.

What does the Bible say about your sin? 1 John 1:9 says that as believers in Jesus Christ, "If we confess our sins, He is faithful and just and WILL forgive us our sins and purify us from all unrighteousness."

We must believe the truth. As the words above confess, God sees us as beautiful and valuable. He sent His son Jesus to die on our behalf so our sins could be forgiven and washed away. Because of Jesus we can have a relationship with God. When we accept the forgiveness Jesus offers, we are restored and our sin is no more. It is a miracle and it is truth.

A lot of people struggle with this because they feel they have to "do something" to earn forgiveness. Reality is, Jesus has done what needs to be done. We can accept His forgiveness in faith believing we have received it. That is where the foundation of our value and self-worth lies. The more you know about who God is, the more you'll know about who you are.

Upon what do you base your belief about yourself? Search out what the Bible says about who you are and how God has forgiven your sins.

25

MORE COOL THINGS GOD HAS DONE

As I stated earlier, we were not allowed to have contact with our first two grandchildren. They were somewhere in Austin, Texas with their father and stepmother. This was a very tough time for us. I saw how hard it was for my wife to cope with this hurt. I remember the day our ex-son in law left with the kids. I had to pry the arms of our four-year-old granddaughter from around the neck of my wife Susan, as that little girl was crying, "I want you to be my mommy". It was heartbreaking. We loved those two kids dearly. At first we hired a private detective from Austin to try and locate them. That did not work out at all. Next, I tried some websites that help you find people and at first that did nothing either.

One day as I walked into the church I saw a picture on our bulletin board. The picture had been there for years but this day it caught my eye. It was a photograph of our grandchildren's last Sunday at River of Life before they left for Texas. The whole church was gathered around them and at that time we told them we would be praying for them. They loved church even at four and five years old. As I was looking at the picture, anger started to well up within me. I thought I had let this hurt and anger go, but no, there it was popping up again. So I went to take the picture down so I did not have to look at them every time I came into the church, which was almost every day.

Once again God spoke to me.

He asked me, "What are you doing?"

I answered, "I'm tired of seeing this picture, we've been praying for a way to see these kids for over three years now, and nothing has happened. It hurts too much to look at it."

God said, "Do you trust Me?"

(Remember I told you God usually speaks to me with questions.)

I answered, "Yes, Sir, I do."

God said, "Then leave it up!"

So I left the picture up and decided to keep on praying that God would open a door sometime for us to see those kids again.

Shortly after this encounter God spoke to me again and told me He wanted me to preach a sermon on Joseph. Joseph who was the son of Jacob, who was hated by his brothers and who ended up being sold to slave traders. You can read about this account in Genesis chapters 37-50. Anyway, one of the points God wanted me to make was how patient Joseph was during this time of trial in his life. God had spoken to Joseph in dreams and told him one day his family would bow down before him and he would save his family. Unfortunately, Joseph shared those dreams with his brothers when he was young and that was one of the reasons they hated him.

I'm going to summarize things that took years to transpire in Joseph's life: Joseph's brothers sold him into slavery. He was falsely accused of trying to sleep with his master's wife, was thrown into prison. Eventually, because of his ability to interpret dreams, he ended up as the right hand man of the Pharaoh of Egypt.

Again, one of the points of the sermon was the patience Joseph displayed. Nowhere is it recorded that Joseph complained along the way. Think about it. God had made promises to Joseph as a young man but most of those promises took fifteen to twenty years to come about. Patience!

When I got done preaching that sermon, God spoke to me and said, "That sermon was for you."

I said, "Father, are trying to tell me it might be fifteen to twenty years before we get to see our grandchildren?"

Again God just asked me if I trusted Him.

Of course the answer was yes. So we just kept on praying.

A few months later I walked into church and again my eyes went to the picture of our grandchildren. And once again I felt the hurt and anger rise up in me, so I started to take it down the second time.

Once again, God spoke to me and asked, "What are you doing?"

And again He told me if I trust Him, to leave it up. So I left the picture on the bulletin board.

About two weeks later I was on a website for finding people and I came across the name, address and phone number of our ex-son in law still in Austin, Texas. After much prayer I got up the courage to give him a call. I got a recording. So I left him a message. Much to my amazement he called me back in a couple of days.

I told him in a couple of months we would be passing through Austin to visit with Susan's brother Don and his wife who lived close to Austin. I asked if it would be possible to visit with the kids just for a few minutes. He reluctantly said, "OK, but just over lunch". We agreed. An hour, we decided, was better than nothing at all.

And the day finally came. We met up with the family on a Sunday at a restaurant in Austin. That day we had lunch with our grandchildren whom we had not seen in almost five years! It went smoothly and we could see the kids were doing very well. The initial meeting went so well that our ex-son-in-law let us spend the rest of the afternoon with the family. In fact he proceeded to tell us that the kids are on spring break from school and would have the week off. He asked how long we would be in the area. We said we had to leave Wednesday. He asked if we would be interested in watching the kids all day on Tuesday because he had no one to watch them for that one day. Of course we jumped at the chance. Wow, God is so good!

Even though the time together went well, shortly after we left for home our ex-son-in-law once again asked us not to contact him or the kids. It seems the kids were asking too many questions that he did not want to answer. So, as I write this, it has been over ten years since we have seen our first two grandchildren. But we are so thankful for the window of opportunity we had to see them for those two days in 2009. We continue to pray that we will see them face to face again. I am so grateful to our Father God for that time. It truly changed my wife's demeanor. She looked like she was ten years younger after seeing those kids and knowing that they were doing fine. Even though I do not agree with our ex-son-in-law's decision to keep the kids from us, it seemed he was doing a good job of raising them. For that we are thankful.

As I have said, many years have passed since that meeting and we have been blessed with other grandchildren. We are thankful to be involved in their lives as much as is possible since most of them live hours away. We are also encouraged as of this writing that contact has been made through Facebook by some of our children with our first granddaughter in Austin. It remains to be seen if this will lead to actually visiting her again. But we are hopeful.

Even though we are not in constant contact with our two oldest grandchildren and have not seen them in the last ten years, that does not diminish the miracles God worked on our behalf. The fact that the one hour we were going to be allotted to see them turned into a half day, then that half day allowed us to be with them for another whole day! Miracle after miracle! That visit was so healing for us and I believe it deepened our faith as well. We had remained patient to see God move on our behalf in this situation. It was pure joy to experience the results of that patience.

What are you being asked to be patient for? How ya' doin?

26

THE POWER OF PRAYER

I believe in the power of prayer and much of what I have already written (or will write) is surrounded in prayer even if I don't specifically mention it. Now let me say this about prayer: It is something we all know we should do because the Bible tells us to do it. Even Jesus prayed.

Often we believe God doesn't answer prayers if He doesn't answer the way we would like Him to. That's really where faith needs to come in. Faith is believing without seeing. Faith also says, "Father, I trust you even if I don't understand or like what's going on." Our God is sovereign and since He knows better than we do, we have to trust and believe when our prayers are not answered the way we expect, that there is a good reason for it and we don't always need to know that reason.

. . .

I remember Sarah, our first-born, asking me to pray about her finding the right guy. She wanted to be married and to have children (if possible because of all the chemo she had as a teenager). Sarah was frustrated and told me, "Dad there are a lot of boys out there but very few men!" She would jokingly add, "My biological clock is ticking and I can't find a Godly man to anywhere." I told her, much to her displeasure, "You are trying too hard. Give it to God and instead of asking 'is this the right guy' every time you meet someone, just enjoy the time and leave the results up to God." So we prayed for God's will to be done in her life whatever that would look like. A couple of weeks later she told me I was right. She had spent time in prayer and told God even though she would prefer to be married and have a family of her own, she was okay being single the rest of her life if that was His plan.

God is good. It was only a matter of weeks later when she called and said that she thought she might have met the man who she would marry, Pete. It all started on a blind date. I could not have chosen a better man. Again there is a biblical principle at work here, which goes back to the account of Abraham and Isaac in Genesis 22 when God asked Abraham to sacrifice his son Isaac. When we are willing to give up everything and surrender our will to God, come what may, usually that is when He is able to give us our heart's desire. Abraham was willing to give up his son in obedience to God, and God provided a sacrifice and preserved Isaac's life. When we give up our deepest desires it shows God that we love Him more than we love what we want.

. . .

At the time I write this Pete and Sarah have been married for almost fourteen years and have been blessed with four wonderful boys. Again, God is good!

What desire do you need to lie on the altar?

27

CRYING OUT

One particular memory of answered prayer came as we were getting ready for a road trip to Illinois to visit Sarah and Pete. It was a Sunday in winter. I'm not sure if it was around Thanksgiving or Christmas, but Susan and I were going to visit for a few days over one of those holidays. We were leaving right after church and the winter weather was iffy. It had been snowing off and on for a few days at this point. So the church family gathered around us to pray over us before we left.

As we were traveling south on US 131 near the Morley exit number 125, I remember this distinctly, we encountered what we found out later was about a 50-60 car pileup. I was in the passing lane going approximately 35 mph. As we came over a slight incline we found ourselves face-to-face with the pileup. The roadway had turned into a sheet of ice. I was following a 4-wheel drive Suburban who suddenly swerved down toward the ditch to the left of the highway and when he did I saw why. The road was impassable because of cars, trucks and trailers all sideways in the road. So I too started toward the ditch to my left. Next thing I knew the Suburban was trying to climb the embankment back toward the highway. It was slowly sliding from side to side, throwing snow from all four tires as it started to climb out. I quickly realized he was heading out of the ditch because at the bottom of it there was nowhere to go. It was either run into other vehicles or run into trees. On the highway there was an opening of about 3-4 car lengths where there were no wrecked vehicles and right on the other side of this opening was the Morley exit ramp. That's where the Suburban was headed, but like I said, it was having difficulty making it up the bank. (He did eventually make it.)

As we slid toward the ditch I told Susan to "hang on because we are going to crash". It was then that I spoke an intensely spiritual prayer: "**Jesus help!**" (Have you ever been *that* spiritual?) That's really all I had time for. Sometimes those types of prayers really are the best, raw and to the point.

Much to my amazement our Chrysler Sebring started to climb the embankment through 3-4 inches of snow, following the Suburban who was still struggling at 4-5 car lengths ahead of us. It was amazing! Our car went up the side of that ditch without spinning a tire. I don't even remember thinking of turning the steering wheel, let alone thinking it would be possible to climb out of there. The next thing I realized we were going across the highway through that small opening of wrecked vehicles and getting off on the middle of the exit ramp. We drove down a few miles and got back on US 131 and finished our trip without incident. Wow, God is so good!

Every time we travel to our daughter's in Illinois we drive past that exit and we thank God for getting us out of that pileup. We look down into the ditch when we drive by and don't believe that our car (which wasn't that great in snow) could make it up that ditch embankment on dry ground let alone in snow of its own power. It had to be God lifting us out of there. I'm still amazed that God would do such a miracle for us. I cannot explain why He does what He does or when He does it. However, I know that Isaiah 55:8 tells us that God's ways are not our ways. In any case, I'm eternally grateful for what He does many times when we cry out to Him.

What miracle do you need in your life right now? Just cry out to Him, raw and to the point.

28

MORE ON PRAYER

One evening I was in the office with a married couple that I had been counseling for some time. The husband was at least twice my size and was dealing with major anger issues. I had been praying for them and with them for a couple of years at this point and was wondering if any of these conversations or prayers was getting through.

During the course of this particular session the husband started yelling and because his wife was tired of being yelled at and wanted distance, she walked out of the room. In his anger, he followed her, yelling at her and calling her names.

Now, I am a patient person for the most part and am slow to anger. But at this moment I felt fury within me. I ran out of the office after him and got between the two of them. It must have been Holy Spirit fire that filled me and gave me the strength to wrap my arms around him as far as possible, pick him up off of the ground (how is that humanly possible?) and set him down in the nearest chair. Then I bent down in his face and said, "Now you've done it, you've pissed me off!" (These words from a man who doesn't curse.)

The man's eyes were as wide as saucers at this point.

I said, "If you ever talk to your wife like that again you will have me to deal with."

That man did cool down and we were able to finish our work together. He never disrespected his wife in such away again, at least not in front of me.

This is not a story about my physical strength, or me losing my cool. (Even Jesus overturned the money changers tables in the temple. Matthew 21:12-13.) It's about how God used this situation to get a large man's attention when it seemed nothing else could.

～

There was a time when I was going through a checkout line at our local supermarket, that God spoke to me and told me to tell the woman in front of me that He loves her. So I said a quick prayer for boldness and obeyed; I told the woman that God had told me to tell her He loves her. As soon as I was done speaking those words, tears started to run down her face and she thanked me. I did not know her and I don't know what impact those words had on her life, I only know that I was obedient to what God was telling me to do at the time, even if it didn't make sense, and even if it was a bit uncomfortable.

.　.　.

We have to be careful not to put God in a box. He alone is sovereign and He can do things anyway He wants to even if it doesn't make sense to us, and/or even if we lose our cool. When we put parameters around God we are limiting Him. We try to understand God through the lense of a finite and fallible human mind/experience, bringing God down to our limited understanding rather than trying to expand our thinking to accommodate the vastness and glory that is GOD.

In what ways could you challenge yourself to expand your thinking and understanding of who God is?

Just like that woman in the checkout line, have you ever allowed yourself to consider how much God loves YOU?

29

A COOL ARMY STORY

A s I had stated earlier, I had rejoined the Michigan Army National Guard to try and make extra income for our family. Initially I thought it would only be for a couple of years and then I would get out. I had a full-time job with UPS, I was pastoring the church, as well as being in the Guard. Before I knew it, time had passed and I was looking at whether or not to re-up. (I had re-upped several times at this point for anywhere from one to three-year enlistments). I was at about the 13-14 year mark of service and I was getting tired of doing all that I was involved in. I thought maybe the Guard should be where I cut back. So as I prayed about a new enlistment I asked God to make it very clear if I should stay in the Guard or just get out by not reenlisting. The time was quickly approaching to make that decision and I needed to hear from God one way or another. Sometimes God will answer our prayers in very different ways. This time the answer came during drills at Camp Grayling, one of the largest military training centers in the Midwest. We were training at the North Camp area. At the time we were a mechanized unit, which means we trained with tracked vehicles called 113's. A 113 is a vehicle that transports 12-15 soldiers to be deployed at another area, usually near a combat zone. The main weaponry for the 113 is a top mounted 50-caliber machine gun.

We were at the North Camp to do night training missions. Evening was approaching and the soldiers were preparing for their training exercise. This exercise included: securing an area, engaging the enemy and firing the 50 caliber machine guns. They were firing blanks with intermittent tracer rounds.

As sergeant, I was ordered to guard an ammo dump (where much of the ammo for the training exercise was stored). I was approximately 40 yards away from the rest of the company who were with 7 of the 113's. The vehicles were parked in a semi-circle in an open marshy area. One of the last things they had to do before they left for their night exercise was to put the firing pins in the 50 caliber machine guns. The soldier selected to do this was a young private freshly out of boot camp. I will call him Mick (not his real name). Anyway, Mick was selected because no one liked doing this particular job. The firing pins had a spring that slid over them as they were put into place. Mick successfully did six of the machine guns, however on the last one the spring popped off and fell into the marshy area near to the vehicle.

I was guarding ammo boxes when I saw many of the soldiers looking through the knee-deep grass of the marsh.

Of course, at this point I had no idea what had happened. Soon I heard the commander yelling quite loudly. Then the troops loaded up into the 113's and departed for the training area where they were going to do their night exercise. The only soldiers left behind were Mick and myself. After the unit had departed I walked over to where Mick was and asked what had happened. He told me about losing the spring and that the commander had ordered him to stay behind and to look for the spring until he found it. Private Mick told me he had no idea where the spring had landed and now the ground was also torn up from the tracks of the 113's. Mick said, "It will take a miracle to find that spring."

Well, I know a God of miracles, so I asked Mick if it was okay if I prayed. Mick knew that I was a pastor and he said, "Go ahead, it can't hurt." So once again I prayed a very spiritual prayer (not really). It went like this: " Father, help! Without Your help we will never find this spring! So, in the name of Jesus, please help!" Mick was about ten feet away from me and after I prayed, I walked forward five steps and guess what I saw? The spring, which is about the size of a spring in a normal click pen, was at my feet ... and it was GLOWING! It was glowing bright neon yellow, like a highlighter used in a book. I was stunned (I'm not sure why), and I looked around to see if perhaps the sun was shining on it to make it glow this way but the sun was disappearing behind the trees. When I reached down into the marsh and touched the spring it went back to its normal greyish color. I realized it was God that highlighted the spring (probably because I would have never seen it otherwise, and also to let me know it was Him that answered my prayer and not just luck that I had found it). Now I wish I had waited to touch it and had told Mick to come over and look at it, because it was so awesome. I picked it up only seconds after I had prayed and called Mick over to take a look. When I told him that it had been glowing, he would not believe me at first. But I told him I would probably never have found it otherwise. Mick said I must have had an extra spring in my pocket to find it that quickly. I told him to think about that. The military does not hand out extra 50-caliber machine gun parts to carry around. I also told Mick that it was a sign from God for me. I explained that I had asked God to show me whether or not I should re-enlist and that I believed this was my sign. Eventually, Mick too believed that God had highlighted that spring for us to find.

Mick and I were alone for several hours before the rest of the unit returned to the area for the night. We talked about God and about Mick's lack of a relationship with Him. I told Mick that God cared about him and his future.

After the unit returned, Mick immediately handed the spring to the commander and proceeded to tell everyone about how Sergeant Fenlon had found the spring after praying and how God had highlighted it for us. The rest of that night and even the next day most of the soldiers stayed clear of me. It was like I hadn't taken a bath for a few weeks. No one got close to me let alone talked to me. I think it kind of scared them, they knew what had happened and also knew it was utterly impossible to find that spring in the marsh. Our God is an awesome God! He is the God of the impossible!

. . .

The next morning the troops had to do an assimilated attack across an open field about 200 yards wide and 300 yards long. As they proceeded in the attack they threw assimilated hand grenades. The grenades were canister-like, kind of like a can of baked beans, with a screw off top. As they ran across the field they would unscrew the tops and throw the canisters in front of them. The grenades would make a small boom and create a lot of smoke. After the mission the soldiers would then police (pick up) the canisters and the tops. As they returned to the assembly area where everyone was supposed to gather there was a count of all the canisters as well as the tops. They had to have every piece accounted for. As they proceeded to count the pieces they found one top was missing. They determined which soldier it was who was missing the top to his canister and told him he would need to go find it.

They asked me (because I had found the 50-caliber machine gun spring) to take this soldier, go back to the field and find the top. We were not to return until we located it. Now I had not witnessed the assimilated attack and when we got to the field the soldier could not remember where he might have thrown the grenade. So, I told the soldier I was once again going to ask God to help. I prayed a short prayer: "God, please help us. In the name of Jesus!" I proceeded to walk about twenty steps into the field and walked right up to the top (it was not glowing). I knew it was once again the hand of God. As we returned to the assembly area my First Sergeant asked me why we were returning so quickly? We had only been gone about five minutes. As I flipped the top to him, he said, "You are the man!" I pointed to heaven and said, "No, He's the man."

. . .

I knew that God wanted me to stay in the National Guard even if I really didn't know why at the time. I often wondered what impact, if any, finding that spring had on Mick. I found out that a short time after the spring miracle that Mick went full-time into the Army.

About twenty years later I got a phone call. It was Mick. He told me he was retired from the military and was getting married. He said that a chaplain friend of his who was supposed to marry them had gotten deployed and could not do the ceremony. He thought to ask me if I would perform his wedding. I told him and his bride-to-be to stop into my office and we could talk about it.

When I met with Mick and his fiancé, the first thing he asked me was if I remembered finding that spring at Camp Grayling out in the swamp. I said, "Of course I do. I've told the account of that miracle many times to many people." Mick told me that miracle changed his life. He went on to tell me he had done several tours of duty in Iraq and Afghanistan. He too was a Sergeant and a platoon leader. Mick said he had told his soldiers the account of the spring many times. He also said, before every mission the men would ask him to pray for safety for them. He never lost one man in all of the missions they had gone on. Now I knew that the spring had impacted Mick.

God is so awesome to be involved in the lives of people who

will just seek Him. The Bible says to seek and you will find, knock and the door will be open. If only we would seek Him. When people ask me if God is real and how they can know Him I tell them what I just wrote: seek Him! If you earnestly do that I know you will find Him. He will show Himself to you. God wants to be found by you more than you will ever realize.

A few years later as I got ready to retire from the Michigan Army National Guard, I was praying about whether to get out or not. I had put my 20 years in and was eligible for retirement pay and health care benefits after I turned 60. I felt it was time to call it a career, but I did ask God to show me what His will was in this situation. My commander and first sergeant wanted me to stay in, however, I really felt like God wanted me to retire.

As I told my first sergeant what I was planning on doing he told me a unit out of Jackson, Michigan, wanted me to deploy with them to Iraq. I told him, no, I was getting out. He said I'd better hurry up and get my 20 year letter (a document that proves I have enough time in to officially retire). A few days later on a Thursday, my first sergeant called me and asked me if I had my letter yet. I told him I did not. He said this unit out of Jackson was no longer asking if I wanted to go but they were going to stop-loss me (make me stay in). If I was going to retire I had better do it that coming weekend when we had drill, but I needed that letter in order to do so.

. . .

The very next day, Friday, I called the National Guard Bureau in Lansing Michigan. I spoke with a lieutenant whom I had spoken with a few months earlier concerning retirement. I explained my situation to her and the possible deployment with another unit, stating that I needed my twenty-year letter ASAP.

She said, "Funny you called when you did."

Reportedly, just before her phone rang she had been looking over the twenty-year letters to be mailed out in the next couple of weeks. She said the next letter she was looking at in front of her was mine! Coincidence? I don't think so. Wow, is God good or what?

I asked her to please fax a copy of that letter to myself and to my first sergeant as soon as she could. The very next morning I had drill. The first sergeant told my platoon sergeant to have me turn in my gear, sign the necessary paperwork in the office and say goodbye to my fellow soldiers. I was no longer in the military. In another day or so I would have been deployed to Iraq. I had told God if that was where He wanted me to go, I would go. But I have got to tell you, riding around in 100-130 degree heat being shot at was not something I felt equipped for at the time. However, I would have gone if I felt God wanted that for me. He did not and made it pretty clear in the end.

When I had retired from UPS, I was told that I would no longer have health insurance but through the military my wife and I would have it for the rest of our lives. Yes, God knew I would need that health insurance and that's one of the reasons He had me stay in even though I didn't realize it at the time. During my twenty years I had the opportunity to do a lot of praying with people and to tell them about my God; the God who loves them and has a plan for their lives.

Do you realize that God has a purpose and a plan for your life?

30

JAIL MINISTRY

I have been blessed to minister to some really wonderful people. God had led me into jail/prison ministry back in the mid 90's. I ministered with one or two other pastors for a few years and later formed a non-profit organization called Northern Michigan Jail Ministry. Through this organization we usually had 10-15 men and women volunteers from various area churches go into our local jail to do church services and Bible studies each week year round.

One couple that we ministered to for many years has come to mean a lot to me. Both husband and wife have great testimonies of what God has done in their lives, and I'm so proud of them as well as blessed to have been a part of their lives. I usually tell people you cannot have a testimony without a test. However, some if not most of our tests are self-inflicted.

.   .   .

This couple, I'll call them Bill and Beth, were both in our local county jail when I was doing church services and Bible studies there. They both had addiction issues and had reached their "bottom". They were going to possibly lose two of their youngest children to the court system because of their poor choices. They were both ready to change their lives because their way of living was not working well. I prayed with both of them to commit their lives to Jesus and continued to meet with them on a regular basis until they were released from jail. They started to attend church and I did my best to encourage them to turn their lives over to God daily and see what He would do in and through them.

I remember Bill would come into church everyday. As I sat in my office I would see him go up on the altar, lay prostrate under the cross hanging there and then I would hear him cry out to Jesus.

"Help me get through today without drinking or using drugs!" he would say.

Day after day Bill would do this. I finally gave him a key so if I wasn't there he could get in. It seemed like this went on daily for almost a year. Then, one day, I didn't see Bill come in, and I asked him where he had been. He told me he didn't need to come into the church, that he started each day by getting out of bed, falling on his knees right there and asking Jesus to get him through that day. As the years passed both Bill and Beth grew in their faith and their love of Jesus, as well as in their sobriety.

During this time I was part of the Jail Utilization Committee (JUC). This was a committee, which had formed due to a need in our community. It focused on assisting challenged individuals to become productive members of the community. I sat on this committee for several years.

At one particular meeting of the JUC were a couple of county commissioners, people from the mental health department, the jail administration, the prosecutor's office and a few other departments that were also represented. I was there to represent the jail ministry. We took turns going around the table giving updates on how our community was faring from the perspective of our office or service. When it was her turn, one woman that I'd known for years who worked to rehabilitate ex-offenders, said, "I just have one question for Pastor Gary. What happened to Bill and Beth?"

What an opportunity to tell people in positions of authority in our community what the Good News about Jesus can do in people's lives. I got to tell them all that the reason people such as Bill and Beth had turned their lives around was because they surrendered their lives to Jesus and were now living for Him. I was so grateful for the opportunity to boast of what our Lord was doing and had done in their lives. I was so grateful to be able to boast on our Lord, and to let these community leaders know that the answer to changing lives was through Jesus.

As I write this, it's been ten years or more of sobriety for both Bill and Beth. Bill has been instrumental in touching many lives for the Kingdom of God by ministering to others through AA, Keryx and Celebrate Recovery. I am so proud of them both for how they turned their lives around by living for Jesus and by serving so many others. What a privilege to have been a part of that.

.   .   .

Is there an addiction you are struggling with? Have you asked God to help you? Are you willing to do what it takes to die to yourself and allow God to transform you into the image of Christ?

31

CHOICES

T hings have not always worked out so well for people I've ministered to. People still have a choice to either follow Jesus and give Him their best, or continue to try to live life their way. As I always say, if you are going to live life your way instead of God's way, good luck.

I have told thousands of people, there is not much in this life I can guarantee, but this one thing I will guarantee you: If you give Jesus your best effort for one year, I guarantee your life will be different in a good way at the end of that year.

It never fails. For those who have taken that guarantee seriously, their lives have been transformed. Why? Because it has to happen! Anyone who sincerely seeks God WILL find Him. That's what the Bible, God's Word, tells us. It is the truth. Seek and you will find, knock and the door will be opened, draw near to God and He will draw near to you. The emphasis is on us to be proactive. God will not force Himself upon us, but He is waiting for us to come to our senses (see the account of the Prodigal Son in Luke 15) and return to Him.

As I mentioned in an earlier chapter, to me, Christianity is common sense. It's based on doing the right thing. I believe God's instructions to us in the Bible are more about doing what is right as opposed to *not* doing the wrong things. Maybe I owe a lot of it to my parents. Perhaps they taught me to always try to do what is right. Perhaps some of it has to do with my childhood. As a young boy and even as a teenager I was picked on (what they call being bullied today) quite a bit because of my small stature. Because of this I have always felt strongly about injustices. So perhaps all of those things I experienced growing up as well as the Biblical influence I received as a teenager, have developed within me the desire to do what is right. Now let's be clear here, that doesn't mean I always DID the right thing. But I knew what was right. In Galatians 6:7 we are told that we reap what we sow. This is a Biblical principle that works for anyone. It's kind of like the saying: "What goes around comes around." If we are treating people the right way, GENERALLY, we will get treated the right way in return. Though there will most likely always be exceptions to the rule.

Unfortunately, the opposite is also true. If we sow the wrong things in life we will receive the consequences of that. I remember one guy who was sitting next to his brother in a Bible study class I was leading in jail. We were discussing this very topic and this man raised his hand. As I called on him, he said, "Pastor Gary, I believe what you are saying is probably true, but I love my sin."

Wow!

"Good luck with your life, my friend," I thought.

The next day that man was released from jail. That man's brother shortly after asked me to visit him in jail. He told me about his life and how he abused drugs. He told me if he didn't change his life that he knew the drugs would kill him. I led him to Jesus on one of those visits. With tears running down his face he asked Jesus to be Lord of his life. He was being released a few days after that and I told him to come to church and I would do everything I could to help him make better choices in his life. When he was released, his brother (the one who loved his sin) picked him up from jail and said, "let's go celebrate your release. I've got some really good drugs..." Unfortunately, the young man chose to listen to his brother rather than making the right choice and within the next twelve hours he was dead from a drug overdose.

I've got to tell you I was as angry as I can ever remember being when I heard of his death. What a waste of a precious life. This young man made a very poor decision by listening to his brother and it cost him his life. I often wonder what the surviving brother thought. Does he still "really love his sin" more than anything else? You reap what you sow and your sin impacts more people than just you. That's why I stress to people that in order to change your life in a positive way it may mean staying away from loved ones, even family members. I will never forget the hurt and anger I felt when I got the news of this young man's death. He was just thirty-three years old and had so much life ahead of him.

Unfortunately, there are many more times this type of thing happened over the twenty-five years of ministry at our local jail. Some lost their lives and others ended up going to prison for many years. If only I could make people see what life could be like if they would only give Jesus a chance. Many times I would say: "What do you have to lose? Give Jesus a chance. Is your way really working out that well?" Yet it comes down to each person making their own choice.

In the jail ministry I used Matthew 7 a lot. In verses 13-14, Jesus says that there are two roads or two gates (or two ways) to travel. One is narrow that leads to life (heaven) and few take it, and the other is broad, the road that leads to destruction (hell) and many travel it. People are either on one road or the other. Or at the very least at the crossroad and wondering which way they should go. I believe Jesus knew what He was talking about when He said most are taking the broad road (which is the easiest way) that leads to destruction. Not only is Jesus talking about eternity here, He's talking about making life choices that could hurt many other people as well.

Your choices don't just affect you, they also affect other people around you. People who care and love you get hurt in the process. Our sins affect so much more than just ourselves.

What is a choice you've made that has negatively impacted others? Ask for forgiveness now. Ask you and you shall receive.

32

ON A GOOD NOTE...

nother pretty cool account from my time in jail ministry was with a man named Tom (not his real name). Tom was a burly guy, not very tall, probably about 5' 8" or so. He was a barrel chested, strong-looking man. Tom was actually kind of scary looking if you didn't know him. He had tattoos everywhere on his body. I first met Tom when he came to a Bible study. God spoke to me that this man had a good heart but needed guidance. So I visited him one on one. I found out Tom had been a skin-head who had hated just about everyone (and probably himself). He even had a tattoo of a swastika on the top of his bald head. As I got to know Tom's story (everyone has a story, everyone has a past), I found out why he was so full of hate. He had been hurt and abused a lot over the years. I told Tom that God had told me that he had a good heart and that Jesus loved him and died for him. Tom eventually committed his life to Jesus. He and I became friends and I visited him while he was incarcerated many times.

. . .

Once during Bible study at the jail Tom said to me, "Pastor Gary I need prayer. There is this guy in here who rides me constantly about being a Christian. I can't take it much longer. One of these days I'm going to lose it and I'm afraid I will lay him out." I told Tom I would pray for the situation. Shortly after that discussion with Tom I felt a strong impression that God was telling him to hang in there. That this was a test of Tom's faith and the man who was bothering him was actually hoping to find that Tom was who he said he was: a follower of Jesus Christ. I told Tom that when the chips were down this man would come to him for strength and comfort. Tom said, "No way, this guy is just being a jerk and doesn't care about anything or anyone." As the next few weeks went on it was getting tougher for Tom to hold back his anger as well as his tongue. One Sunday as I was preaching in the jail, Tom asked me to come visit the next day. He said he was at the end of his rope with this guy and he could not take it anymore. I agreed and told Tom I would visit the next day so that we could pray together for strength and wisdom to get through this. Then I reminded Tom of what I had said earlier, that the day would come when this man would turn to him if only he could keep his cool.

The next day I went to visit Tom. He walked into the visitor's area with a smile on his face. I hadn't seen that smile in a few weeks because of what he'd been dealing with. Tom told me, "Pastor Gary, it was just like you said!" He went on to tell me that it was late the night before while he was reading his Bible, that along came this "jerk". Tom immediately asked God to give him patience and to help him not hit this guy. The man stood in front of Tom and began to cry. He told Tom that the corrections officers had just informed him that his father had passed away. He asked Tom if he would pray for him. Then he said to Tom, "You're the only real Christian in this jail."

Wow! Look, I'm not smart enough to give Tom the advice I gave him. It had to be wisdom from the Holy Spirit. However, it all came to pass just as I had told Tom it would. As Holy Spirit had told me it would. Tom was amazed. I reminded Tom, "What if you had lost it, if you had hit the man or if you had verbally let him have it? Who would he have to go to for prayer and comfort?" I often wondered later what impact that had on the man. Would this man give Jesus a chance in his life because of how Tom had handled himself? To this day I don't really know. But I do know that Tom, who faithfully attends church, has told me he has seen this man several times in the last few years, and every time he has approached Tom with a handshake and hello. I pray that man always remembers how Tom reacted to his ridicule and perhaps will ask Tom why he responded the way he did. Then Tom can tell him more about Jesus.

You can't always choose your circumstances, but you can choose how you go through them. What circumstances are challenging you right now? What choices will you make?

33

MORE CHALLENGES

S ome people I have spoken with over the years
seemed to think because I had a close relationship
with my God through Jesus Christ, that nothing bad
would ever happen to me or my family. As I have already
written about some of the challenges our family has faced
over the years, we still have situations and tests we face from
time to time.

Jesus said in John 16:33:
"In this world you will have trouble,
but be of good cheer,
for I have overcome the world."

One of the latest tests we faced, again involved cancer. In
January of 2014, my wife Susan, was diagnosed with breast
cancer. As the doctor told us the results of the biopsy, we
both were a bit stunned. The doctor's bedside manner was

not the best and our conversation with him seemed to bring fear to the surface.

The doctor urged us to immediately schedule surgery and chemo. We indicated that we needed time to pray and process the diagnosis before deciding what course of action we would take. As we exited the doctor's office I was praying for wisdom and for words to use to comfort my wife. A scripture immediately came to mind, (it's always good to hear the truth of God's Word). The verse was: "We have not been given a spirit of fear, but of love, power, and a sound mind," 2 Timothy 1:7.

Susan and I talked as we left the building and immediately made the choice not to be afraid of the news we had just received but to trust God and see what He had for our future. I remember Susan saying: "What's the worst that can happen? I die and I go home to be with God."

Isaiah 55:7-8 immediately came to mind: "God's ways are not our ways, and His thoughts are higher than our thoughts."

After much prayer and research, we decided to treat the breast cancer naturally. The cancer was in stage 2 and we felt there was time to try an alternate treatment.

I was so proud of how Susan fought the cancer that was trying to invade her body. She implemented a regiment consisting of a strict diet, along with exercising, as well as taking some natural supplements to strengthen her body to fight off the disease.

For about one year Susan did very well with the plan she was following. However, at the end of that first year our oldest daughter Sarah was again diagnosed with cancer, breast cancer. Sarah has written a book entitled Finding Myself ... Facing Cancer that is all about her experience concerning her breast cancer journey if anyone would like to know more. Once again, we knew we could choose to either trust God with whatever came our way or not.

All I will say about it is once again I was so proud of my oldest child. Sarah did a lot of research before making her decision to go forward with treatment. And again, she attacked the disease head on. I know it was painful, stressful and challenging for her, but how she went through it was amazing.

After Sarah was diagnosed and eventually went through surgery, Susan was helping with the four boys. Over the course of several months Susan made herself available to watch the kids and to support Sarah throughout her recovery.

It seemed once the dust settled with Sarah's latest cancer battle, Susan found she had lost ground in her own battle with breast cancer. Almost two years after being diagnosed we found her cancer was progressing. We decided to get another opinion on a course of action. We chose Cancer Treatment Centers of America (CTCA). The closest location was north of Chicago in a small town called Zion.

We were very confident in the treatment protocol laid out by a team of doctors and specialists at CTCA. They were very thorough and informative about how to approach breast cancer treatment.

Almost two years to the date of the diagnosis of breast cancer, Susan and I were at CTCA. The first day there she was put through a variety of tests by the various departments. I especially remember the last test of the day, whereby a brain scan would be done. It was toward the end of a long day. The appointment in this department was scheduled for 4:30 PM and they were pretty much right on time. The scan was supposed to take about 25-30 minutes. At about 6 PM I was starting to get really concerned as to what could be taking so long. I was the only person left in the waiting room, which had several people seated in it just an hour before. Even the receptionist had gone home for the day. I prayed and asked God to give me peace, but the minutes just dragged on. Finally, at about 6:50 PM. a nurse came out and asked me if I was Gary, Susan's husband. She told me to come with her. All I could think was: *What is going on?* As I was escorted into an examination room, I found a technician along with Susan waiting there. The technician proceeds to inform us that we could not leave the hospital. After doing the brain scan the results showed a couple of spots on Susan's brain and he did not feel he could allow her to leave. I immediately started praying in my head asking God for wisdom and peace. The technician had made a phone call to Susan's primary doctor at CTCA and he finally made the decision to let us leave the hospital and return to our hotel room for the night. We had to return the next morning to consult with Susan's primary doctor as to what to do next.

After consulting with Susan's doctor, we were sent to see a brain surgeon that worked closely with CTCA in a city about 25 miles away. After visiting with this specialist, brain surgery was scheduled for the very next day. Talk about a whirlwind! Here we were in a hospital we had never been to before, in a place far away from home, to figure out how to battle breast cancer and now Susan was being scheduled for brain surgery! It was definitely a time of testing of our faith.

To make a very long story short: Susan had the brain surgery and it turned out fine! No cancer as the doctors had suspected.

As Sarah was ending her treatment Susan was just beginning. Throughout the coming months Susan went through treatment: chemo, surgery and radiation. She dealt with the cancer with such faith and strength. I was (and am) so proud of my wife.

Even though it was a difficult time for our family, once again our gracious God proved himself faithful in so many ways. It was His care, provision and guidance that helped us through. If you are facing a tough time in your life, I encourage you to ask God to help you, then allow Him to do so.

Who do you turn to in your tough times?

Perhaps the most important question you can ask yourself is: If you were to die do you know where you would spend your eternity?

34

MORE COOL STUFF GOD DID

One morning a friend of mine, Roy, gave me a call. Roy was a bit bewildered because he could not find his wallet. It was not where he always put it when he goes to bed for the night. This particular morning the wallet was not where it was supposed to be. Roy told me how he had looked everywhere and torn apart drawers and had run out of places to look. He asked if I would please pray for him to find the wallet. So we prayed together and hung up. A couple of minutes later Roy called me back. He found it! The interesting part was that he had found the wallet in the exact place he first looked, however, it had not been there then. How can one explain that? I cannot, but all we can do is thank God for putting it there to be found.

~

I'm a sports nut. I enjoy almost all types of sporting events. I used to get a newspaper of which I especially loved the Sunday Edition because the sports section was very large. I couldn't wait to get home after church and sit down and spend 2-3 hours reading that newspaper and scouring the sports section, which contained information about all the teams in all the different sports. One day as I was sitting in my easy chair sipping on an iced tea and engrossed in my sports section, out of the blue God spoke to me. He said: "Do you know you are spending more time reading that newspaper than you are with me?" Wow, that hit me like a ton of bricks. I loved reading the newspaper but I had no idea I had let something as simple as that come between God and I. The very next day I cancelled my subscription to the newspaper. That was over twenty-five years ago now. Look, there's nothing wrong with reading the newspaper. There are a lot of other innocent ways to spend our time. However, if we let anything become more important to us than our relationship with our Father God, then we are wrong. I still love sports and love watching them. I have told God if I am watching too much, or if it's getting in the way of our relationship, just let me know and I will walk away immediately. So far, things seem to be pretty well balanced.

~

God speaks to us in many different ways. He answers prayers in many different ways as well. Some of those ways are unusual. One such answer to prayer came about in the life of one of the single woman in our church. She was having furnace problems in her home. The furnace would not stay lit. So, she had a man come out to inspect the furnace. He told her she was lucky to be alive, that the furnace was malfunctioning so badly she could have died from the gases that were not being vented properly. He immediately shut it down and told her she needed a new furnace. As she gave a testimony at church of how God had spared her life, she also asked everyone to pray for the finances to replace the furnace. Being a small church, we were in no position to assist her in buying another furnace. We prayed with this woman for almost a year asking God to help with finding and funding a furnace. I helped her to check on used furnaces, and we tried to find anyone willing to give her a break on a new or used furnace. But it was all to no avail. Nothing seemed to work out. So we kept on praying for God to make a way. We prayed for her safety as well, because she was using several electric heaters to keep the house at least warm enough so the water pipes wouldn't freeze. Northern Michigan winters can get pretty cold after all. I tried the best I could to encourage her every week to trust God and to keep praying. I would tell her that somehow God would meet her need for a new furnace. Week after week we would pray together in faith and ask the church family to keep praying that this need would be met.

After about a year I happened across an advertisement in our town paper about a contest that was being held by a local heating and cooling company. They were offering a free furnace along with free installation for someone who was especially in need. The requirements were that a friend, pastor, etc. would write a letter to this company stating why this person or family was in need of the furnace they were offering. I jumped for joy. I quickly got a letter out to this company explaining the need of this woman. We then prayed for the right person to be selected no matter who that may be. We were informed a short time later that the lady from our church was the winner of the new furnace. Wow! God is good and He can work in mysterious and amazing ways, including a contest!

What cool stuff has God done in your life?

35

ORDINARY GUY . . . EXTRAORDINARY
GOD

I can't honestly say I know why God would choose to use an ordinary man like me for His extraordinary purposes, except that He does it all the time. Scripture says, in I Corinthians 1:27, God uses what we would perceive as foolish to shame the so-called wise. The Bible is full of such examples. But what I can say with all honesty is that each time God has shown Himself in my life, each step I have taken and chosen to submit to Him, has only served to deepen my faith and trust in Him. These are examples from my life, examples of my faith. But, why does that matter? It's truly not so important what I think. It's not so important what your family thinks or your friends. The most important thing is what God thinks. We must always return to God and to His Word for truth, for guidance and direction. I hope you've been encouraged and inspired through the telling of God's amazing grace in my life.

These accounts of His awesome love are not only for me to

share and experience, but for you as well. Perhaps you are one such ordinary guy or gal and you wonder what God might do in your life if you let Him. I encourage you: surrender. Allow God to show you the depth of His love for you and the height of His creativity and extraordinary power.

AFTERWORD

Well, when I started writing this book I said, "I don't know where to start."

Now I'm at a loss on how to end it!

When I reflect upon my life and how good God has been to me, I am in awe. As I write this, I've recently retired as Pastor of River of Life Church after twenty-one years and as President of Northern Michigan Jail Ministry after fifteen years. I was remembering my time in both of those ministries with a friend of mine and we realized through the twenty-five years of jail ministry alone, I've probably ministered to around 40,000 men and women. If we add in preaching over the last twenty-one years at River of Life Church as well as other occasions in different churches, I've had the honor of preaching to probably over 100,000 individuals. Wow! Considering this leaves me to wonder: who am I to have had this privilege? God is truly good.

Many have asked me, "What's next for you now that you are retired?"

I can honestly say, "I don't know. However, I know it will be good."

I know that because it is God who is in control. I do know that Susan and I will be spending a lot more time with our grandchildren. Hopefully, we will be a positive influence in their lives. We will enjoy the journey that God has laid out before us.

I pray that somehow what I've written will be a blessing and an inspiration for the "average" person to trust God. Just know that if God can use a guy like me, He can (and will) use anyone who will invite Him to. Give Him a chance; you never know where it will lead.

Who knows, you might even write a book about all of His amazing works one day!

www.ingramcontent.com/pod-product-compliance
Lightning Source LLC
Chambersburg PA
CBHW070810050426
42452CB00011B/1970